Buy Low, Sell High, Collect Early
and
Pay Late

The Manager's Guide
to Financial Survival

DICK LEVIN

Associate Dean
School of Business Administration
University of North Carolina

Buy Low, Sell High, Collect Early and Pay Late

The Manager's Guide to Financial Survival

GINGER TRAVIS
contributing editor

LAMBERT DER
artist

ECHO POINT BOOKS & MEDIA, LLC

Published by Echo Point Books & Media,
www.EchoPointBooks.com

ISBN: 978-1-62654-924-1

Cover design by Adrienne Nunez,
Echo Point Books & Media

Printed in the U.S.A.

To my brother, **Bob Levin,**
who gave me both advice
and financial support
when I needed them most.

Contents

Contents

Preface

This book is about money: how to get it, how to use it, how to collect it, how to pay it, how to count it, how to compare how much of it you've got with how much the other person has, and how to keep a reasonable proportion of it from the IRS. If you're a CPA, it will hold little attraction for you (except for the cartoons). If, instead, you are a person who must deal in financial matters, though with a shaky background, my prediction is that you will find this book both useful and enjoyable (including the cartoons).

I've used a light, often irreverent style to explain some pretty heady financial stuff: asset management, performance analysis, cash flow vs. profit, how to borrow more from your banker(s), how to put money in a business the smart way, how to grow fast without going bankrupt, effective income tax strategy, and how to choose and use tax and accounting professionals. These are all topics that managers in business need to understand well but often don't.

In this book you'll read about the financial escapades I have had with some of my friends, and maybe some of yours too! We'll see successes and we'll see failures. And we'll learn how to avoid the latter.

Lots of folks leave their mark on a book like this: my editor Ted Jursek at Prentice-Hall, his encouragement; my very able production editor Joan Foley, her patience and advice; Lambert Der, his marvelous art; and Ginger Travis, her invaluable editing, input, ideas, and most of all her friendship. To each of these people I owe a special debt.

But in truth, most of the inspiration for this book came from a secondhand furniture dealer named Jess Max for whom I tuned pianos during college. He came to me one day and said, "Kid, just remember: *Buy low, sell high, collect early and pay late.*" You know the rest . . . . . . enjoy.

DICK   LEVIN

Chapel Hill, N.C.

Buy Low, Sell High, Collect Early and Pay Late

The Manager's Guide to Financial Survival

ONE

Looking Back,
Looking Ahead

Argent, geld, okane
Tiền bạc, para, raha,
Pénz, peníze, pieniądze
Dinero, dinheiro, danaro

What smells as sweet by any other
name?

Money

Last time I counted, there were 268 basic books in accounting, 167 finance texts still in print, and 300-odd volumes on subjects ranging from *How to Make a Million Dollars in Your Own Small Business* to *What to Do First in Bankruptcy Court* and *Investment Strategies for the Coming Millennium.* For $1.75 to $22.95, the curious reader could learn from the "experts" how to beg, borrow, steal, invest, and manage the stuff that entrepreneurial dreams are made of. *Money.*

If, like me, you fall for the allure of those promising titles every time, you've got Peter Drucker at the office, John Train on the bedside table, Howard Ruff in the head, and Jane Bryant Quinn under the Christmas tree (and God knows what forgotten effluvia in the basement). And now there's this Dick Levin out front banging on the door. What, O Lord, another one? Deliver us from writers!

I guess I've read, taught from, recommended, and left on planes and in rented cars at least half of the legitimate stuff in accounting and finance, not to mention piles of the how-to-get-rich-at-home-in-your-spare-time, change-your-life-forever, be-a-winner, avoid-probate-cure-warts-and-psoriasis, full-satisfaction-or-your-money-back-guaranteed genre. There are junk money books exactly like junk food; there's Michelin four-star writing at the other extreme; and there's a smorgasbord in between. Something for every appetite. The next time *you* want some bedtime reading guaranteed to put you away, get hold of any academic journal of finance or accounting and put your 20/20s to work on an article like "Lagged Beta Weight Differentials as Predictors of Interim Cyclical Variation in Leverage Ratios." This beats barbiturates, but given a choice, I'll take *How to Make a Million Dollars in Your Own Small Business* any day! (And pass the Doritos while you're up.)

READERS I HAVE KNOWN, OR
MIRROR, MIRROR ON THE WALL,
SEE ANYBODY YOU KNOW?

For the undergraduate business students where I teach, the University of North Carolina at Chapel Hill, there are more different basic accounting and finance texts available in the student bookstore than there are total games in regular and postseason basketball play for Dean Smith's finest. And guess which are in greater demand. (Hint: There's never been a documented case in UNC history of a scalper's sale of *Introduction to Cost Accounting.*) So what do business majors read and retain? Well, given brief exposure to any of the four-dozen solid textbooks available (title page and table of contents the night before the final), adequate sorority and fraternity quiz files, occasional class attendance (nothing that could be construed as obsessive), uncounted cases of Miller and Stroh's, and a good run of luck, our undergraduate men and women come away from the business school with, at minimum, an expanded vocabulary ("LIFO/FIFO," "discounted cash flow," "point guard," "playing the low post") and a practical appreciation of statistics ranging from the unemployment rate just before their graduation to Carolina's field goal and free throw percentages in the prior three ACC basketball playoffs.

Ten years later: Spouse, kids, two cars, and second or third rung on the institutional ladder. Reading matter: *The Wall Street Journal, Fortune,* and (secretly) *How to Make a Million,* etc. Financial how-to books are written for that market segment comprised by the legions of

3

salaried managers who dream of owning and running their own wildly successful businesses — as opposed to filling five days a week, fifty weeks a year, until after fifteen years of continuous service uninterrupted for any reason other than military obligation or extended sickness they accrue three weeks of paid vacation. These are good people who help the wheels go round. They audit payroll accounts, assist new car buyers filling out loan applications, become assistant manager of the West Oshkosh branch of Flexiwidget International, and buy how-to books in the airport after missing the fourth connecting flight this month between their customer's plant in Sioux City and Storm Lake, Iowa. (Some of them/us even teach undergraduate business students their new words and buy how-to books while secretly yearning to do deals instead of articles for the *Journal of Finance*.)

Well, why not feed the dreams that feed the authors that fill the bookracks that revolve in airports coast to coast? Dreaming about making your first million sure beats dreaming about earning your age in thousands. (And, besides, I have this *great* idea for an airport bookstore franchise operation, biggest thing since B. Dalton, motor-driven bookracks, our own line of how-to guides by in-house writers, tie-ins with the airlines, gateside seminars for business travelers at all the major airports, cassettes, video disks — we'll clean up — and I'm writing a book on how *you* can do it at home in your own spare time.)

THE BUY LOW, SELL HIGH GANG

Well, there *is* one other group, but I'm not sure all of them read, at least not textbooks or how-to books. These are the men and women who have the knack without the knowledge, who can do it but can't explain it, who know they're making a pot of money but can't cipher whether it's a 15 or a 50% return, who know how but not why, who listen to but find it hard to talk with their CPAs, who sometimes sense that something is wrong financially with their business

but not exactly what or where, or who just plain need to know how to work effectively with financial ratios and concepts in their own enterprise.

If You're One of Them, Have We Got a Deal for You!

The buy low, sell high gang has the instinct of entrepreneurship — of "doing business" — but some lack formal training in accounting and finance. Others may have been exposed to formal accounting and finance at that age (eighteen to twenty-two) when they blithely traded discounted cash flows, internal rates of return, financial leverage, ratio analysis, and working capital management for beer and boogieing — which may have been an age-appropriate substitution then, but holds mighty cold comfort now when their banker shoves a prime plus 5% factoring note across the desk for them to sign while mumbling something about their asset turns being in the lowest quartile of the *Robert Morris* studies.

If that scene in any way captures your consternation (and some of your aspirations to acquire financial knowledge), then you are what they refer to as the "target market" for this short book, I really don't care how much money you have (or whether you have any for that matter). What I do assume about you is the following:

1. You are in business or have a real plan to get into business, with the mindset to back it up.
2. For reasons not important here, your formal knowledge of finance is lacking.
3. The operational meaning and practical significance of accounting and financial ideas is much more important to you than their research origins.
4. Your schedule can accommodate ten hours to read this book — then ten more to read it again carefully.
5. Bankers and CPAs generally irritate you with their language, their business philosophy, and their personalities. (Generally, I say, because there are exceptions to everything, including maverick CPAs who own and run businesses.)
6. Approaches to teaching and learning with lots of anecdotes

and examples turn you on more than lists of definitions and principles.

7. You have made and lost enough money somewhere to have the humility necessary to make lots more.

8. Short words and plain talk are the way to keep your attention.

If this short list fits you fairly well, read on. We may have something in the following chapters that will help you to reach your goals.

CASH FLOW IN AN EARLIER LIFE

My father Meyer Levin was a traveling salesman for much of his life, right down to the 1936 Ford coupe. He sold fruit and vegetable packaging, things like bushel baskets. During WW II (as both Pop and Archie Bunker were fond of saying), my father sold lots of bushel baskets to peach growers in the sandhills section of North Carolina. Since the basket truck deadheaded home empty, he had this great idea of sending a couple hundred bushels of peaches back to me twice a week to sell retail in our little town of Williamston, North Carolina. I was thirteen at the time (you know the age) — long on ideas, energy, and self-confidence, but short on brains and judgment. And if accounting and finance existed in those days, I'd never heard of them.

Well, I was too young to drive a truck myself, so I hired a tenant farmer named Sim Bell who had this terrific 1942 Dodge pickup. Sim and I would cruise the back roads of Martin County all day selling peaches to Sim's friends (and he had a million). Since the economic institutions of eastern North Carolina decreed that all these good folks got paid at the end of tobacco season (August), and since Sim vouched for their credit, I saw nothing wrong with doing most of our business on credit. And so I did — with a vengeance.

After two weeks — four loads of peaches — my father returned home and asked me for "an accounting." A

7

what? I remarked that business was great and that we had made a profit of nearly $800 (four truckloads at 200 bushels each, sold for a dollar more than he paid for them, less spoilage, truck expenses, and what we ate). He was delighted with the news and asked me where I had deposited the money; I showed him my bank balance of $65. He was dumbstruck. I was puzzled. It had never occurred to me that businesses recognized income on anything other than my primitive idea of the accrual basis, that is, Sim and I immediately rejoice over profits on peaches sold, delivered, and eaten by his friends in July, surely to be paid for after August. My father, who knew something about bookkeeping and a lot about human nature, spent the rest of the day explaining to me why I was having so much trouble paying for the gas for Sim's truck and our sandwiches for lunch even as I was making a killing in the peach business. My appreciation for cash flow was born at that moment. My credit policy changed drastically the next day.

UNCLE LOU ON CAPITAL
FORMATION THEORY

My mother Minerva Levin had a brother Lou who owned a corner Frankfort Unity Market in Philadelphia. This was your typical neighborhood grocery. The time was 1940 and such stores would soon be in their death throes, strangled slowly by the new supermarkets. We were living in New Jersey (before we moved south), and it was the family custom to gather Sundays in the back of Uncle Lou's store, where his family lived. If we were extra good, Uncle Lou would take us kids into the store after lunch and let us pick out whatever candy we wanted from the world's biggest glass candy jars (to ten-year-old eyes). Uncle Lou always handed out philosophy with candy. One Sunday he said, "Dickie, always remember, it takes money to make money." I was more interested in the treasures in those glass jars than in Uncle Lou's business philosophy. Many years later as I studied the relentless encroachment of the well-capitalized chain supermarkets on what had been the exclusive turf of family-owned, underfinanced grocery businesses, I realized how much of capital theory and forecasting were captured in Uncle Lou's experience and his simple statement, "It takes money to make money."

Uncle Lou died a poor man, his Frankfort Unity Market having long since been replaced by a shiny new A & P store. So what do you bet Uncle Lou is looking down at A & P's agonies right now and laughing like hell.

So much for the origins of Levin's concepts of capital formation and cash management. (Bet you have a few of your own like that — there's no knowledge like personal experience.)

MENU

As any proper book should, this one begins with fundamentals.

- In Chapter 2 we'll run balance sheets and income statements by you fairly rapidly. Our aim there is to minimize worrying about picky little stuff like what goes on what line and how many spaces you indent, and concentrate instead on (1) differentiating between the myths and realities of financial statements and (2) learning how smaller businesses "diddle" on financial statements; that is, how their statements mingle personal and business affairs and how their accounting tends to reflect family practices more than it does business performance. And (3) why it therefore takes more than one set of books to know what the hell is really going on, as well as to survive bankers, the tax authorities, and the competition.
- With fundamentals under our belt, Chapter 3 addresses the question, "Where do we get the money we need to do all the wonderful things we know we can do?" Here we examine (1) sources of financing, (2) equity versus debt financing, (3) venture capital markets, and (4) the care and feeding of your banker(s), with special attention paid to the topic of how to get more money out of your bankers.
- Chapter 4 is a primer on how to put money in your

business the right way — so that you can get it out again. Emphasis is on (1) why you may need to keep the family and business separate, (2) whether you should take stock or notes for money you put in the business, (3) the right way and the wrong way to own real estate, (4) how to profit from 1244 stock, and (5) how to save money with family real estate partnerships and leasing companies.

- Chapter 5 dives right into the question, "How are we doing as a business?" We'll show you, step by step, how to compare your business with similar businesses. Just as in a physical examination, we begin with measuring vital signs, move through recognizing symptoms, get to the point of diagnosing illness if one exists, and finish with a recommended regimen of treatment.

- Chapter 6 discusses the first of three of the most nagging financial problems faced by smaller businesses — that of how to finance a rapidly growing company without owning (or robbing) the Bank of America. Here we'll work on ways of curbing your business's appetite for outside money as it grows.

- In Chapter 7 cash flow is our subject. We'll begin by differentiating profits from cash flow, then demonstrate how these two behave in different growth and financial situations, point out some ways of solving cash flow problems, and finally show what inflation does to cash flow and to profits.

- Chapter 8 treats the third financial problem facing smaller businesses, getting money out of the business without being eaten alive by taxes. We'll talk about designing salaries, dividends, and bonuses to minimize the total tax bite. Then we'll work on getting appreciated property out of a corporation without paying back all the delicious gain to the IRS. Buying out family members, swaps, and the new issues market are also treated in Chapter 8.

- Chapter 9 concerns the strong working relationship between the owner-manager of a smaller business and his or her accounting and tax professionals that is a requirement for strong growth and wealth creation. And yet, in far and away the majority of cases with which I am familiar, this kind of relationship just doesn't exist. Chapter 9 concentrates on the psychology of the relationship between managers and financial "experts." We will discuss (1) how to get "them" to work for you, (2) the different tax and financial postures you can take and the consequences of each, (3) the methods (and costs to you) associated with financial conservatism, and (4) how to win the tax game if you decide you want to.

A BOY NAMED SUE, OR BERNICE
ON BANKERS AND ACCOUNTANTS

If you could measure street sense, then the smartest MBA student I had in twenty years was a young man named Bernice (who already came equipped with enormous aplomb from having dealt so long with his odd name). Bernice understood accounting, cash flow, return on investment, working capital use, and everything else we taught in the MBA program. But his real strength was that he also understood deep in his gut the role accountants and bankers were put here on earth to play. In Bernice's model, accountants and bankers were tools for managers to use — and like any tool, each had a specific task. Bernice maintained that bankers had all the money and accountants were the folks you used to get the money from the bankers. He believed neither of the two knew a damn thing about running a business and only a fool ever let them get involved in running one.

When Bernice finished the MBA program he had $400 cash and an old car. It took him three years to find the business he really wanted to buy, by which time he was down to $100 and the same old car. The asking price was $850,000 with $250,000 cash down. It took him a year to buy this business, and he finally did it with no money down either. Three years after that, Bernice had made a half-million dollars from his business, pretty nearly tax free.

Now the point of this story is *not* that he made money — hell, a million people do that every day. Nope, the point is that Bernice used three different accountants to apply to nine different banks before he found an accountant with an approach that rang some banker's bell, so he could buy the business with nothing down, and then take a half million out tax free.

R.S.V.P.

If using accountants to ring bankers' bells and starve the IRS is to your taste, stick around for the banquet, there are more courses to come. On the other hand, if that sort of thing turns your stomach, there's this very edifying article you could look at, "Lagged Beta Weight Differentials . . . ."

Still with me? Say grace, and let's get on with the first course.

"Grace."

TWO

An Accounting Primer: Myths and Realities

> *. . . in conformity with generally accepted accounting principles applied in on a basis consistent with that of the preceding period.*
>
> *– Representative Wording, Auditor's Report*

> *Consistency is the last refuge of the unimaginative.*
>
> *– Oscar Wilde*

First We Eat Our Spinach

"Accounting? Ugh!" Please, no groans, Accounting 101 was never so good for you. Skip this chapter only if you've already had seven courses in accounting, made A's in all of them, understood everything that was said, believed less than half, and have begun three or more businesses successfully. (You may also skip this chapter if your name is Peter F. Drucker.) Everyone else — including you CPAs and bankers — should read this chapter twice.

THE BALANCE SHEET

We begin our accounting primer by looking at the balance sheet. The balance sheet turns out to be nothing more than a snapshot of the financial condition of a company *as of a given day.* The balance sheet is not a motion picture, or a history, or a forecast. Therefore, it does *not* show how the company got to that condition on that day, and it does *not* show where the company is heading. It simply puts a frame around one day and shows where the company is — right now.

Parlez-Vous Accounting?

The accounting profession has its own vocabulary and conventions. Not all of what they say is true, and not all of it makes sense. But it always balances, and everybody in the profession uses the same words, and two out of four ain't bad for starters. Now, to make some good practical sense out of what the accountants tell us, we first disarm them by learning a few key words of their language. *Allons!*

Balance Sheet Logic

A balance sheet describes the financial condition of a company in the same way that you would describe your personal financial condition. First, it lists the company's financial resources, such as goods and property and the money other folks owe it, under the heading *assets.* Then, it lists all the debts the company owes to other people and calls them *liabilities.* Then, it subtracts the liabilities from the assets and calls the difference *net worth* or *equity.*

What you own less what you owe is what you're worth. For keeping track of this incredibly complex algebraic relationship, your CPA charges you $100 per hour. So much for balance sheet logic.

An Instructive Example

Let's say that you have $500 in the bank, an old car worth $1,500, and a house and furnishings worth $30,000 on which you owe a $15,000 mortgage. Suppose that you currently owe $50 to the guy who keeps your old car running, $120 on your credit-card bill from last month, and $30 for this month's utility bill. Your personal balance sheet would look like this:

Assets		
Cash	$ 500	
Old car	1,500	
Cheap house	30,000	
Total assets		$32,000
Liabilities		
Mortgage on cheap house (probably at 5%, you lucky devil)	$15,000	
Repair bill owed on old car	50	
Master Charge bill	120	
Light bill (as they say in the country)	30	
Total liabilities		$15,200
Net worth (If you got $16,800 as the answer here, read on; if you didn't, we need to have a talk)		
Net worth		$16,800

Is It Any Different for a Company?

Nope, just a few more zeros after the numbers; the logic of the balance sheet relationship stays the same for your company as for yourself:

What it Owns Less What it Owes is What it's Worth.

However, for good reasons most companies like to keep track of these three things in a bit more detail. So we see company balance sheets that look more like the following than like the abbreviated statement you just encountered.

Bay Area Corrugated Pipe is a real company I've worked with; the numbers are rounded for convenience.

BALANCE SHEET
Bay Area Corrugated Pipe, Inc.
December 31, 19X2

Assets

Current assets			
Cash	$ 560,000		
Marketable securities	80,000		
Accounts receivable			
(net of est. bad debts)	4,600,000		
Inventory	7,200,000		
Prepaid expenses	160,000		
Total current assets			$12,600,000
Fixed assets			
Land		200,000	
Fabrication shop			
and office	2,500,000		
Furniture	50,000		
Trucks and			
machinery	1,700,000		
		4,250,000	
Less: Accumulated			
depreciation		1,050,000	
Net fixed assets			$3,200,000
Total fixed assets			$ 3,400,000
Total assets			$16,000,000

Liabilities

Current liabilities			
Accounts payable	$4,420,000		
Notes payable	1,930,000		
Accrued expenses	280,000		
Long-term note			
(current portion)	700,000		
Total current liabilities		$ 7,330,000	
Long-term liabilities			
Mortgage note payable		2,800,000	
Total liabilities			$10,130,000

Equity

Capital stock	$ 500,000		
Retained earnings	5,370,000		
Total equity			$ 5,870,000

Quick — Does It Balance?

Bay Area Corrugated owns assets listed on its balance sheet of $16,000,000 and owes liabilities of $10,130,000. Its net worth is the difference between these two figures, $5,870,000. (Net worth is also known as stockholders' equity in a corporation.) The arithmetic checks out, but don't get all fired up over mathematical accuracy — bankruptcy courts are full of mathematically accurate statements from certifiably defunct companies.

My father was in love with statements that balanced. In his later years he had a small wholesale business. He was easy prey to accountants because he looked at "balances to the penny" as the true test of accounting worth. His accountants could spend half a day combing his books to find a 10 cent error, then charge him their full rate for doing it. He delighted in paying them for such stupid effort. It was a kind of sacred trust; they were duty bound to find the 10 cents, and when they had, all was right with God and Pop's books.

A few days after he died, we were in his office trying to make sense out of Pop's books. You couldn't find out a damn thing from them, namely, what he really owned and what he really owed. But, by God, they were in balance — to the penny, of course. Are you listening, Pop?

Naming the Beasts

To portray the financial condition of a company, it isn't enough to deal with total assets or total liabilities. Classifications this broad don't give us sufficient information about what's going on. Therefore, it's common practice to break down these classifications into smaller ones.

Take, for example, the section titled *current assets*. Current assets include cash and other assets that we expect to turn into cash in the near future, and near means within a year from the date of this balance sheet. Total

19

current assets for Bay Area Corrugated Pipe are shown as $12,600,000. Let's look at them one at a time.

Cash — is exactly that. If you have any money in the bank or lying around your office, you enter it here. Bay Area has $560,000. Wonder what they're going to do with all that.

Marketable securities — is cash that you may have invested in securities like T-bills to earn money during the time you don't need it. Usually, we show these on the balance sheet at what they cost us. Bay Area tells us that it owns securities that cost $80,000. Let's hope the market is up.

Accounts receivable — represents money our customers owe us for work we've done for them. We always enter this figure as a *net* amount; that is, we first subtract money we don't think we are going to be able to collect. Why? Not only is the result more accurate, but subtracting anticipated bad debts also cuts taxes. The IRS lets us deduct money we can't collect — or *say* we can't collect. Netting out bad debts from receivables has nothing to do with balancing, but it is always a good thing to do any time you can. Bay Area says folks owe $4,600,000 that Bay thinks it will collect. We certainly hope so.

Inventory — represents materials Bay Area uses in the manufacture of pipe, both pipe being made in their shop and finished pipe sitting in the yard but not yet shipped. The $7,200,000 Bay lists here represents the lower of (1) its cost or (2) market value. Yes, this is a conservative way to list inventory. But you have probably guessed by now that, if they are anything, CPAs are conservative.

Prepaid expenses — this one is slightly weird. Suppose that on July 1, 19X2, halfway through the financial year (the uptown word for which is fiscal year), BAC paid a year's premium on its casualty insurance for the entire company. If this premium had been $320,000 and six months later if on the day we cipher up our balance sheet, December 31, we still have half a year's insurance paid for, we call that prepaid, and list it as worth $160,000. Thus, prepaids are payments already made, from which the company has not yet received all the benefits it has coming in the current accounting period. Better we should remember this item as "half-used-up insurance policies," OK?

So much for *current* assets. We now know that Bay Area Corrugated claims that it has $12,600,000 in cash and other assets it can turn into cash soon.

Fixed Assets — What's the
Matter, Can't They Move?

Trucks are fixed assets, yet they move. Accounts receivable are current assets, yet they stay in a fixed location. So sue me, it gets worse. *Fixed assets* represent assets that you do not *intend* to sell. (Not that you wouldn't sell in a flat minute if somebody offered you enough money.)

The fixed assets section on the balance sheet includes

> *Land* — which is entered here at what you paid for it, even if your granddaddy bought it from the Indians for $24 and called it New Amsterdam. Bay Area bought theirs for $200,000 and it's called Clearwater, but it's home to them.
>
> *Buildings and equipment* — get different treatment from land. The fabrication shop, furniture, trucks, machinery, portajohns, and mobile barbecue are carried on the balance sheet at *net fixed asset value,* which is what they cost when they were built or bought, less the *depreciation* that has accumulated by the time you cipher up the balance sheet.
>
> *Depreciation* — is the decline in the useful life of an asset due to wear and tear, time, rust, new inventions, wars, atomic bombs, falling off the back of trucks, and pretty much anything else than can happen to it. When Bay Area, Inc., spent money to build its shop and office, buy furniture, and purchase trucks and machinery, it decided the cost would be spread over the expected useful life of the assets. Thus, *each* year can be charged with a part of the fixed assets.

For instance, if Bay Area bought a light truck for $20,000 and it was expected to last three years, Bay would charge $6,666 depreciation each year for three years. One year after Bay Area bought the truck, its balance sheet would show

Truck	$20,000
Less: Accumulated depreciation	−6,666
Net fixed asset value	$13,334

See how simple it is? Now of course if it really wants to know what the damn truck is worth, all Bay has to do is put an ad in the newspaper and try to sell it; this is cheaper than using a CPA at $100 an hour, but newspapers don't do your taxes for you.

OK, so we total up all the fixed assets and they come to $3,400,000 for Bay Area Corrugated, Inc.; add this to our $12,600,000 of *current assets,* and we can say with mathematical precision that, on December 31, 19X2, Bay, Inc., had total assets of $16,000,000. Are you wondering how much faith we should put in balance sheets done on New Year's Eve? Take heart. Maybe CPAs don't celebrate New Year's Eve like the rest of us.

As They Reap, So Shall They Owe

Liabilities are broken down into categories in all balance sheets, too, just as assets are. *Current liabilities* are debts that will be due within a year from the date of this balance sheet — $7,330,000 in the case of Bay Area, Inc. This is the other side of the coin from current assets. We get the money to pay our current liabilities from our current assets — more about this relationship and what it means for good financial management later.

> *Accounts payable* — Bay Area Corrugated, Inc., lists accounts payable of $4,420,000; this is what it owes to the folks who sell it stuff on credit.
>
> *Notes payable* — this entry of $1,930,000 means Bay owes this much money either to a bank or some other lender.
>
> *Accrued expenses* — this is the side of the coin opposite to prepaid expenses. At any point in time, including the day on which the balance sheet balances, Bay Area owes salaries and wages to folks who work for it, interest to folks who lend it money, and fees to CPAs who cipher up

all these numbers. Any such debts that have not been paid go here under accrued expenses. Bay Area tells us it owes $280,000 here.

Current portion, long-term debt — it's a fairly common practice to include under current liabilities *this* year's portion of any long-term debt that the company owes. That's so the company can see what is coming due within a year and that's why Bay lists $700,000 under current liabilities as the current portion of its long-term note.

Total up all the above and you get $7,330,000 — that's all the money, as of December 31, that Bay owes and expects to pay within a year. (Of course, if CPAs really do celebrate New Year's Eve, maybe there's something they forgot to list?)

The Longer They Give You to Pay
It Back, the Better

Many companies are lucky enough to be able to borrow money for longer than a year, and that's usually a good deal any time they can get it. Bay owes somebody $2,800,000, evidenced by a long-term note. This debt goes in a different place on the balance sheet from current liabilities, probably so that Bay won't worry as much about it as it worries about money it has to scrape up within one year.

Total up current and long-term liabilities and you get $10,130,000, which is all the money Bay Area Corrugated owes — and that's a bunch, isn't it?

What You Own Less What You
Owe Is What You're Worth

Fine. If Bay owns assets of $16,000,000 and owes debts of $10,130,000, then it is worth $5,870,000. Earlier we called this net worth or equity. Equity can be broken into two parts. In the vernacular of the street, we call these parts "put-in equity" and "left-in equity."

From the $500,000 entry in the equity section of Bay Area's balance sheet, we know that someone *put in* $500,000 of capital (either to start the business or after it got going); the fancy — or $100-per-hour — term for that is *capital stock*. The *retained earnings* figure of $5,370,000 is nothing more than the sum of all the profits left in the business since it began (after taxes and dividends were paid). Although Bay has retained earnings of $5,370,000, it has only $560,000 of that in cash. Where is the rest? Well, somewhere on the balance sheet — we hope.

The Chi Phi fraternity at our university had a professional audit done, the $100-an-hour variety, that came up with a retained earnings figure of $7,500. This disclosure so excited the brothers that they authorized the purchase of new furniture for the house in the amount of $7,500. Fact was, however, that their cash account was something nearer $100. Now if they had had a few business majors as members rather than all those prelaw, political science majors, the brothers would have known the difference and have avoided embarrassment. (If you believe that one, you don't know nothin' about business schools, and you sure don't know nothin' about fraternities.)

THE BALANCE SHEET — REALITIES

Things are seldom what they seem, and that goes double for balance sheets. The goal of this section is to go back through the balance sheet in the same order as before and look at the realities this time. One word of explanation before we begin this trip. The difference between myths and realities in the balance sheet has multiple causes:

1. *Time.* Even when the rules are applied consistently, time, inflation, and the vagaries of certain marketplaces all make assets and liabilities behave in strange ways; there's little we can do about that.
2. *Diddling.* Some folks "diddle" with their balance sheets.

Things that belong there don't get put there, and things that don't belong do get in there. People diddle for lots of different reasons, the two major ones being to impress bankers with how financially strong they are and the IRS with how financially poor they are. Especially in smaller family-controlled companies, balance sheets that have been diddled with tend to merge the family and the corporation to the point that, after years of being diddled, the balance sheet doesn't tell anyone much about either the family *or* the company that makes sense.

One other thing: diddling comes in two varieties, legal and illegal. I encourage you to diddle legally to the maximum extent possible. That's just good sense. If you want to talk about illegal diddling, you better talk to someone else. I know a few people who have done time in Montgomery, Alabama, for illegal diddling.

3. *Incompetence.* Some folks have — and there is no nice way to say this — damn poor accounting help. When this is your problem, you can be a saint about diddling, you can be wholly free from the ravages of inflation, but your balance sheet over time will still get less and less useful. Read that as farther and farther from the truth, where truth is still defined as "what you own less what you owe is what you're worth." You can do something about this problem: show your accountant the door and get some savvy new help.

Current Assets or Realities
I Have Known

Cash is cash. What you see on the balance sheet is what you get. It's hard as hell to make cash where none exists; when you or your auditor verifies your bank balances, that's about it. Although it won't buy as much as it used to, you can pretty much take the cash entry on the balance sheet as gospel.

Marketable securities are another thing entirely. Remember, accounting rules (the $100-an-hour word is *conventions*) require you to carry marketable securities on your balance sheet at what they cost you. Suppose that you bought a thousand shares of Genentech stock for your company when it came public at $6 a share and it is now $240 a share. (If it isn't, don't carp — we can dream.) Your balance sheet entry under marketable securities ($6,000) is now $236,000 shy of the truth.

What to do — change the entry to $240,000? Heaven forbid, that's against the rules. But now that I have your attention, let's think for a minute about the value of having a *market value balance sheet*. A market value balance sheet is exactly what its name implies, one on which things are listed at what they're really worth, not according to what someone else's rules say they're worth. Does that mean you can get rid of your $100-an-hour "regular balance sheet" (known in the trade as an *historic value balance sheet*)? No, don't tear it up yet. There are still folks like the IRS who require historic value balance sheets, and, besides, if you report to the public you must report that way. There are even some people out there who still actually believe in and support the historic value balance sheet idea. Some of them are CPAs. Will wonders never cease?

What I Owe Ya, Preacher?

I once employed a local Baptist minister, Paul Stevens, as a farm manager. Paul used to delight us with his stories of mountain behavior. One day a young man and his "woman" walked down out of the Tennessee hills to Paul and asked him to marry them, which he did with his customary good humor and grace. When the ceremony was concluded, the young man asked in hill language, "What I owe ya, preacher?" Paul replied, "Whatever you think is right, young man." Whereupon the young man reached in his pocket, picked out a quarter, and gave it to Paul with "I be grateful to ya, preacher."

On the balance sheet, we have to be a bit more careful about what folks owe us. Bay Area Corrugated, Inc., tells us that its accounts receivable (net of estimated bad debts) are $4,600,000 on December 31. In Preacher Paul's parlance, that ain't gospel; it's an estimate at best, because it makes some very explicit assumptions about the collectibility of those debts. Since the IRS lets businesses "charge off" bad debts either when they go bad or as a percentage of accounts receivable based on some history, it behooves Bay Area (and us) to be pessimistic about collecting. After all, if a doubtful account, previously charged off, does pay us in another year, we can always declare it as income and pay the tax then. In the meantime, we get an inch ahead of the IRS.

Although the IRS allows folks to charge off bad debts (and early too), many companies just don't. Consequently, their accounts receivable entry on the balance sheet cannot be taken at face value. Then, too, many customers have disputes with companies about what they owe. Disagreements are fairly widespread in contracting, for example, but the balance sheet isn't set up with space for disputes.

Conclusion: If you want to know exactly what folks owe you, don't look on the historic value balance sheet. Review each account, make a determination of whether or not it is collectible, match this against your past history of collecting, adjust for "disputes outstanding," and then add it up and see what you've got. Anything else is nothing more than a guess. If what you get is far from what you show on your historic value balance sheet, then all the more reason to consider a market value balance sheet for a better crack at the truth. Oh yes, I forgot for a minute, folks diddle here too. Remember when you sold your brother-in-law a riding mower for $1,600 last spring? Come on now, you know you're never going to dun him for the payments; go ahead and write it off. Take your loss (and your tax deduction) like a man — well, like a brother-in-law.

*Beans, Beans . . . Who Can Count
All the Beans?*

Inventory is another slippery little devil we have to deal with realistically. To find out whether you made any money, you have to calculate something accountants call *cost of goods sold.* In a very simple example, it goes like this:

You tell them you started the year with an inventory of	$ 1,000,000
You tell them you bought widgets, gidgets, and gadgets for	+3,000,000
	$ 4,000,000
And you tell them your year-ending unsold inventory of widgets, gidgets, and gadgets is	−2,500,000
You have thus defined the cost of the widgets, gidgets, and gadgets you did sell as	$ 1,500,000

Very neat, very precise, and very accurate. Hold on, pardner! Look at the role the year-ending inventory plays in this calculation. If it's lower than $2,500,000 (say, $2,000,000), cost of goods sold will be $2,000,000 and profits will be correspondingly lower — and taxes will be lower too, don't forget. And if year-ending inventory is $3,000,000 (instead of $2,500,000), cost of goods will be $1,000,000 and profits will then be correspondingly higher — with higher taxes too!

And just who determines exactly what the value of inventory is? You do, friend! "Oh," you say, "but I have my books audited every year." So did the man in New Jersey (De Angelis was his name) who claimed to have about $100 million in salad oil that simply was not there. And then there's my friend in Kentucky with an inventory of over 12,000 different items (that really are there) whose real value fluctuates so rapidly that probably he is the only person in the world who can state with certainty what they're worth.

Now what's the point of this harangue? Just this. If the inventory entry on your balance sheet has such important consequences for reported profits (and therefore taxes) and if its real value is the subject of a judgment call, then we can easily see how its balance sheet value is sometimes the subject of diddling.

"Well," you say, "I simply wouldn't do anything like that." Fine, I say, but do you remember what we said earlier about inventory being carried on the balance sheet at the lower of cost or market? Good, then just suppose that last year, right before the price doubled, you bought a million board feet of lumber for $200 per thousand board feet. It's on your balance sheet now at $200,000, but it's really worth $400,000. What to do? Can't change the historic value balance sheet — rules is rules. But what about your brand-new *market value balance sheet?* Remember that in rapidly changing times — inflationary or deflationary — a market value balance sheet is the *only* sensible way for business people to keep up with reality. Look at it this way. If you wanted to borrow money on that lumber inventory of $400,000, would you still claim to your banker that it was worth only $200,000? Gotcha! Would he insist that you claim it was worth $200,000 when you know better? If you say "yes," then what you need is another banker.

Conclusion: Cipher up your historic cost balance sheet for those who love it or need it or believe in it. Then turn around and make yourself a current *market value balance sheet* too. There is no other way to keep score accurately, and someone in your company needs to know what's *really* going on. Why not you?

*Fixed Assets Get Accounting
Diseases Too*

Land, land, they jes ain't makin' any more. I remember when a farmer in South Carolina used that line on me to justify an outrageous price per acre for a farm I wanted. And by gosh, he was right! Land is carried on the balance sheet, using $100-per-hour rules of course, at *cost.* No matter what has happened to it. The owner of Bay Area Corrugated, Inc., shows land on the balance sheet at $200,000. This land happens to be twenty acres near downtown Clearwater, which would bring $1,500,000 at an auction with only one bidder. Clearly, Bay Area's balance sheet net worth is *understated* by $1,300,000.

Solution: You want to change the land entry to $1,500,000 so that it reflects reality? Yes, and you die at dawn if you try it, too! Rules forbid that sort of thing. But

again, take heart — just carry it on your *market value balance sheet* at what it's worth. If anyone gives you a hard time, get an appraisal (you can probably get one for less than $100 an hour at that).

Now suppose Dame Fortune deals you a really rotten hand. Read, you bought twenty acres of swampland near Clearwater that was to be drained and developed, and you got it for a bargain, only $10,000 an acre. Then along came hurricane Izell and your swampland is ocean now. The IRS and CPAs to the rescue. If you can prove it's worth nothing, you can change its value on your balance sheet from $200,000 (what you paid for the swamp) to $0. And there's more — you can take the $200,000 loss off your taxes too. Well, why in hell don't they operate the other way too and let you show the world that your land is worth $1,500,000? You can, you can — just sell it for $1,500,000 cash, pay a lot of taxes, and show the rest on your balance sheet under cash. Now, wouldn't you rather work on a *market value balance sheet?* I'm with you! Nuff said.

The Older It Gets and the Worse
It Looks, the More It's Worth
and the Longer It Runs
(Depreciation in Reverse)

What did we say about depreciation a few pages back? Depreciation is the decline in the value of an asset. My friend at Bay Area Corrugated Pipe, Inc., bought this Transtar, a big gorgeous eighteen-wheeler truck, two years ago for $76,000. He ran it and depreciated it for two years, then found out this spring it was worth $78,000 as a used truck. So much for balance sheet depreciation. So much for controlling inflation too!

Conclusion: The net asset value on the balance sheet is the result of applying a mathematical rule to the purchase price and has nothing to do with the realities of what things are worth. If you want to find out what they're worth, advertise them for sale and see who calls. To maintain a balance sheet that reflects the real current value of fixed assets, prepare a market value balance sheet. It may not be as precise as an historic value balance sheet, but it sure as hell is a lot more accurate!

Diddling Revisited

Plants and offices are a favorite diddling place for folks, especially those in the lumber, contracting, and construction supply businesses. Lots of people in these areas have a habit of "expensing themselves" a new fixed asset. Or, put more simply, they use their own labor and materials and build a new warehouse, plant, or office without ever putting it on the balance sheet. That's sort of dangerous diddling, but it's done nonetheless. The market value is there right on the lot, but not on the balance sheet. People in the general aviation business and in trucking often rebuild engines (using their labor and parts), but they don't put the rebuilt engine on the balance sheet as they should. Contractors buy pumps and charge their entire cost to a single job (quite legally, I might add). When the job is finished, they own a perfectly good pump, but, you guessed it, it isn't on the balance sheet.

What to do? Simple. At a minimum keep a separate notebook with what you own and what it's worth this afternoon. If you want to do more, invest some real effort in making a market value balance sheet. It's the best thing to do if you want good practical information, and it's legal too. The best thing about it is that it makes sense even if *you* are the only one who ever looks at it.

But Ain't That Old Historic Value Balance Sheet Good for Something?

We used to be able to say that, if the balance sheet did nothing else right, at least it did show the true balance of what you owed. Sad to say, those days are gone too!

For sure, the balance sheet does a good job of reflecting accurately accounts payable. But then, even if it didn't, your creditors send you accurate reminders each month (at no accounting cost to you, I might add). Notes payable to banks and other lending institutions are the same — just miss a payment and the bank is right on your tail. But what if the note is payable to you or your partner?

It's common knowledge among CPAs that the notes payable section of the balance sheet of closely held corporations tells as much about equity as it does about debt. Now what does that mean? Just this — you can put your money in your corporation two ways, by taking stock or by taking a note. When you take stock for the money, the accounting entry gets made down in the stockholders' equity portion of the balance sheet. When you take a note from the corporation, the accounting entry gets made in the liability section of the balance sheet. Your money doesn't care; it arrives in the cash account either way.

Just try, however, to *take* money out of a corporation. That's another story entirely. If you took stock ten years ago when you put the money in, it will be as hard as hell to get your money back out again without paying through the nose in taxes. If, however, you took a note for the money, it will be a breeze to get your money back tax free.

See? *That's* the reason we can't trust the balance sheet here either. Much of the debt represented under the liability portion may in fact be equity money put in by principals who were savvy enough to know that that's the right way to put it in if they ever intend to get it out and still have some left. More on this in Chapter 4.

One final note about mortgage notes (due and payable). Many corporations rent their buildings and lease their equipment from family-owned partnerships. This practice is exactly what should happen, and we'll have more to say about it in Chapter 4, too. When buildings and machinery get bought and sold between the family and the corporation, legal diddling results *as long as the price reflects fair market value.* But items bought and sold at prices that in no way reflect the true value of the asset distort the corporate balance sheet. Of course, these transactions may also do very nice things to the family balance sheet.

Conclusion: If your diddling includes the buying and selling of assets between the family and the company on "favorable terms," any similarity between the corporate balance sheet and reality will be purely coincidental. Do your corporate self a favor and keep a separate, real-world balance sheet.

A successful automobile dealer in our area was audited by the IRS a few years ago. On his balance sheet, he showed a substantial entry representing a quarter mile of woven wire fence complete with barbed wire top. A clever field auditor picked this up but could not remember seeing such a fence as he entered the property. A search of the corporate premises that morning failed to turn up any such fence. A quick ride by the owner's palatial country estate, however, disclosed a fence suspiciously like the one on the company balance sheet. Alas, greed got in the way of common sense and led to a substantial settlement with the IRS. Could it have been accounting error and not greed? Probably not. As much grief as I give accountants, they do know the difference.

THE INCOME STATEMENT (A.K.A. PROFIT AND LOSS) — MYTHS

If the balance sheet is a picture of the financial condition of a company as of a given day, the income statement is a record of a company's activity for an entire period. Often, the period is one year, but income statements can be prepared covering any period, including a month, a quarter, or a half-year of time. The income statement matches the money received from selling the stuff you make against all of the costs you incurred to make it. This comparison shows whether or not your company made a profit.

Income Statement
Bay Area Corrugated Pipe, Inc.
Year Ended December 31, 19X2

Gross sales	$24,800,000	
Less: Returns and allowances	800,000	
Net sales		$24,000,000
Expenses		
Cost of goods sold	19,100,000	
Depreciation	680,000	
Sales and administrative expenses	2,690,000	
Total expenses		22,470,000
Operating profit		$ 1,530,000
Less: Interest		910,000
Net profit before taxes		$ 620,000
Provision for income taxes		300,000
Net profit after taxes		$ 320,000

*Is There Any Money
in the Corrugated Pipe Business?*

Our income statement for Bay Area Corrugated Pipe, Inc., covers the period from January 1, 19X2 through December 31, 19X2.

This statement tells us that, in 19X2, Bay Area, Inc., sold $24,800,000 worth of pipe, allowed its customers $800,000 off their bills for returned pipe and such, and wound up the year with $24,000,000 of net sales. The company states here that the cost of goods sold was $19,100,000, that it also incurred depreciation of $680,000, and that it spent $2,690,000 for selling and administration. Subtract the $22,470,000 expenses from the $24,000,000 net sales, and you get what's called operating profit equal to $1,530,000. Farther down the statement it reports paying $910,000 in interest (we remember from the balance sheet that it does owe quite a bit of money), which, subtracted from the operating profit, gives a net profit before taxes of $620,000. The IRS clipped Bay for $300,000 (it's clear that Bay Area needs to read the later chapters of this book), leaving it with an after-tax profit of $320,000 for the year's work. Whether that's good or bad we'll leave for later. Here we are interested only in how you get the number. All pretty straightforward, so far.

INCOME STATEMENT — REALITIES

Now You See It, Now You Don't

You would think that sales is sales and that's that — just bang the pipe together, load it in a truck, send the bill, get money back, go to the bank with money, come home, and light a fat cigar. Uh oh, not so simple. (It never is.)

The $24,000,000 net sales Bay, Inc., reports represents only the net amount it *billed* customers, not what it *collected*. To use $100-an-hour lingo again, Bay Area recognizes income on the *accrual* basis. Using the accrual basis of accounting means that you put things in the column when they are *billed, not* when they are collected. And most businesses operating today use this method. So, Bay's $24,000,000 of net sales doesn't have a hell of a lot to do with what's in the bank (which you may remember is cash, and that's found on the balance sheet). The entry for $24,000,000 means only that Bay billed people $24,000,000 in a year, not that it collected same. The difference is important. Remember Sim Bell and me in the peach business? All those sales and no cash?

Accrual-basis recognition of income is commonplace; and so is another reality, legal diddling. . . .

Leads and Lags
as the Economists Say

Suppose Mr. Bay, Inc., decides late in November 19X2 that his taxable income for 19X2 is already too high (lucky devil), and here he is with more than a month yet to go. He makes a couple of phone calls to customers who are to receive $2,000,000 of pipe in December and a deal is struck. He'll deliver the pipe on schedule — in

December — but delay the billing until January 19X3. Ergo, Bay's income statement no longer reflects what was actually sold this year. Funny thing, neither does Mr. Customer's income statement. "Ought to be a law against this," you say. Nonsense, the IRS lets you average income to reduce taxes. All Bay, Inc., has done is to average its income, and, I might add, without spending a dime on accounting fees.

Now look at another situation. It's late November again, and Mr. Bay is looking back over a dismal 19X2 for profit. There's no real chance to change the profit performance materially in the one month remaining, and he's promised his banker the moon in 19X2. Oh, doctor, can this line of credit be saved? Well, maybe. Mr. Bay makes a couple of phone calls to customers having a particularly good year, and once more a deal is struck. Bay will bill the customers in December for pipe it will ship in January 19X3, and for its trouble will give the cooperative buyers another 4% off the price.

"Hey, just a good business deal," you say. Fine, but the point I'm making is that "deals" like these, though legal and profitable, ruin the ability of the income statement to reflect what really went on in 19X2 (or in any other period for that matter). If you do "deals" like this, and want to make year-to-year comparisons of sales, costs, and profitability, don't plan on getting your information from a single diddled income statement or you'll diddle yourself. You will have to keep another notebook of what you really sold. Or you might invest in another income statement.

You think trying to keep a grip on reality is driving you crazy with all these notebooks and income statements? Look at Bay's banker with one diddled income statement. You know the guy is smart if he's got ulcers worrying about reality vis-à-vis Bay and other similar commercial accounts. If he's fat and happy with the statements they feed him, and sleeps like a baby at night, then he's *dumb.*

Building contractors for years were the ultimate users of this now-you-see-it-now-you-don't, leads-and-lags income-reporting strategy. Under the IRS code, contractors used to be allowed to report income on the "completed contract basis," which means you don't report nothin' until the job you're building is completed. Until the IRS got wise, lots and lots of jobs just never got "finished," and millions and millions of tax dollars were never paid. The IRS may be slow, but they sure are relentless, and they finally came out with a rule saying that when 95% of the estimated job cost has been billed the customer, the job is finished — no excuses, no arguments, by God it's finished, now pay us the tax and shut up. That pretty much scotched the contractors' "free lunch," but contractors are tenacious too. If you don't believe it, why are December and January the two months during the year in which more construction jobs get "finished" than any other months? Think it's the fine construction weather we have then? No, silly, it's just contractors exercising their leads-and-lags, now-you-see-it-now-you-don't, poor-man's tax-averaging, bank-confusing, income-reporting strategy — and all legal too. And now the government wants to do away with the completed contract method, pity.

Who Is Us, Who Is Them?

The most common transgression against realistic accounting in closely held corporations is confusing the family finances with the corporation's finances. If IBM, General Motors, and Exxon aren't guilty of this practice, it's probably because they can't figure out how to get away with it, not that they wouldn't like to. Let's get right down to Mama's mink and Dad's Mercedes sports coupe with a short truth test.

Q: Under cost of goods sold, how many relatives work for the company? I mean the ones who are too young, too infirm, too old, or too dumb to do a real job. Gotcha!

Q: Who uses the Beechcraft Baron 58 TC more, the family or the corporation? Gotcha again!

Q: What members of the family drive Porsches, Mercedes, and Cadillacs from the company motor pool but don't turn a hand for the corporation?

Q: Who in the family besides the president of the corporation went along on the last trip to Brussels to the trade exposition and served coffee in the exhibition booth an hour every morning for "appearances" sake?

Q: Why is the rent the corporation pays for the family-owned warehouse 25% higher than the going commercial rate?

Q: Why is the president's father (age seventy-five) living in Sarasota, Florida, and drawing $2,000 a month as a company consultant?

Enough Gotchas

I think we can agree that a family-owned and -run corporation is not a true stand-alone accounting entity, no matter what the president says. And, therefore, its income statement reflects more the "way of life" of the family and corporation combined than it does a true accounting of what the company sold, what it paid out, and what it had left when the period was all over. And, listen, I only laid on you a half-dozen of the more common gotchas; I know a hundred more besides.

So, what's it mean for us? Just this, the fact is that income statements may reflect any number of different things from a small company's performance to leads-and-lags, now-you-see-it-now-you-don't company accounting to combined corporate/family life styles. If income statements measure all these at once, how can anyone really measure how the *company* is doing? No way.

Conclusion (a lecturette): If you engage in any or all of these nefarious practices, don't look to me for approval or criticism — a moralist I'm not. But don't look to me for help either in figuring out who sold what to whom and when. I wasn't there when you did it! Ready for the moral? *Keep some records that make sense,* at least to you.

We had a sawmill operator near one of our farms

years and years ago. His name was Howard and he kept his records on a wooden shingle. Howard knew *exactly* how he was doing; his grip on the reality of his business was flawless.

WRAP-UP AND SCORECARD

Things to remember about accounting myths and realities:

1. What you see is *not* necessarily what you got.
2. Whether the balance sheet actually balances is not the real issue.
3. Inflation undermines democracy and the accuracy of the balance sheet too.
4. Diddling may be legal or illegal, moral or immoral, but diddling without keeping the right records is just plain stupid.
5. Balance sheets based on historic cost cannot help us years later. (If you are into history, buy a damn history book — no, better yet, let the family buy it and you rent it from them.)
6. The only way to tell if the inventory is there is to go count it yourself. If you've done that already, you probably know what inventory means to reported profits.
7. Income is income when it's billed, except when you can't collect it, except when you didn't intend to collect it, . . . except when you've changed your mind about the relative you sold the riding mower to anyhow.
8. Always write off bad debts before you think you should. Shows poor faith on your part about human behavior but helps win the tax battle.
9. The smarter you become in buying low and selling high, the less accurately your balance sheet reflects your acumen.
10. If you diddle yourself up a new plant by using labor and materials, don't put it on the balance sheet, silly.
11. Debt is different from equity except when money that should have been put in the company in exchange for stock is exchanged for notes — except when you never intended to take it out again, in which case you have not read far enough in this book.
12. If you rent to your family, make them sign a long lease and always charge them more than anybody else — they are generally poor tenants.
13. If you want a fence around your beach house, don't buy it with company funds. Let the fence dealer use your prop-

erty free for ten years to test the corrosive-resistant properties of his fencing.

14. Bill them this year and collect next year, or bill them next year and collect this year . . . do anything you want but collect the money, dammit!

15. Cheating the IRS is fun — until they catch you.

16. Cheating the IRS is dumb whether they catch you or not — there are too many ways to do it that are legal.

17. Remember, when all else fails, buy low, sell high, collect early, pay late, and keep your books on a shingle. You know the rest.

THREE

Dealing with Bankers and Other Folks Who Have the Money You Need

> *Let me tell you about the very rich. They*
> *are different from you and me.*
>
> *– F. Scott Fitzgerald*

> *Yes, they have more money.*
>
> *– Ernest Hemingway*

I grew up in a one-horse North Carolina town called Williamston. It had one bank, and in those days I could write a check in Raleigh where I went to college, spend the proceeds of that check for two weeks, and then go home to Williamston and put enough money in the bank to cover the check and still have a day or two to spare. Oh for pre-electronic banking days and good old float. Today, my kids can write a check on Monday, put the money in on Tuesday, and pay the returned-check charge on Wednesday.

Anyhow, in Williamston our one bank was actually a commercial banking and venture capital establishment all rolled in one. There was the regular bank, and then lounging around the front lobby every day there was Frank. Frank was a rich old coot, and he loved making money; he was Williamston's first venture capitalist. The bank, on the other hand, was ultraconservative and hated to risk a nickel. The bank made you put up a dollar and a quarter collateral for every dollar borrowed, with a loan-to-deposit ratio probably not more than 40%, and the bank manager had authority to lend up to $1,000 without calling the loan committee together. Standing in the lobby, Frank would catch every person who had been turned down for a loan as he left the bank, and he'd structure a loan to fit that person's situation. Frank had no restrictions on interest rates, terms, loan-to-value ratios, or what you wanted to do with the money — build a mechanical crabpicker or pay off gambling debts. But just let you be one day late paying and zap, that's all she wrote. Frank foreclosed like a beartrap. He repossessed and sold collateral for twenty-five years — farms, cars, buildings, inventory, everything but grandma and the kids. Frank died a multimillionaire with assets probably exceeding the bank's. And he rarely lost on a deal. Frank had an intuitive grasp of what my colleagues in finance call "risk-return analysis in secondary financing markets." He was a natural.

CARE AND FEEDING
OF YOUNG BANKERS

And Not a One Named Frank

About 30% of the MBAs coming out of our program go into banking, most with regional banks, and a very few intrepid souls with the investment banking houses of New York and Boston. You should know more about this 30% of the MBA class because you're going to meet them over and over again (if you haven't already had the pleasure). They're the custodians of the money you need.

The regional bankers our MBA program turns out compare with the rest of their MBA class this way:

Intelligence	Average
Initiative	Below average
Aggressiveness	Below average
Creativity	Below average
Self-reliance	Average
Personal appearance	Above average
Greed	Bottom of the pile
Risk-taking need	Bottom of the pile

There are of course a few exceptions every year, but on balance the bankers we train fit that profile and seldom surprise us. Banking appeals to these men and women because it offers a cocoonlike environment, lots of structure, well-developed support systems, and all the opportunity anyone could ever use to avoid risk-taking decisions. Banking is a very safe industry; it's hard as hell to go bankrupt in a bank. Take a look at the bankruptcies over the last quarter century (even the 20 in 1982); compare that with any other industrial group. You really have to be a first-class twit to go belly up with a bank.

Risk and Return

Ah yes, the Lord giveth and He taketh away. Bankers are not paid much. Notice that I didn't say bankers are underpaid. They are definitely not underpaid given the low levels of risk they usually assume and the jobs they do. A good house painter with a helper can make more than the average banker. I have an MBA graduate in Charlotte, N.C., who began with a brush in one hand and a sprayer in the other; he's now a commercial painting contractor and makes more than any banker in the state — more, in fact, than any MBA graduate in his entire class.

Levin's First Rule for Dealing
with Bankers

Never approach a banker as you would another businessperson. That is a dumb, possibly fatal, mistake. If there's anything that bankers *are not* and *do not* understand, it's businesspersons and business. (Would you run your business the way bank trust departments run theirs?) No, bankers shy *away* from business from the time they are in school.

On the Job Training: Analyzing
Ratios and Perfecting Your
Handshake

Generally, the first six months bankers spend on the job is given over to a training program — or retraining in the case of MBAs. They are taught accounting all over again, financial ratio analysis, how to pick apart a customer's historic value balance sheet using *Robert Morris* (more on this book later), ways to determine how much a customer can pay back, and hundreds of other numbers-oriented problems — but not one face-to-face standard two-pair-bluff confrontation in the whole damn training period. Just numbers, numbers, numbers.

Young bankers also get graded on how well they fit in the organization — everything from well-shined shoes and a firm handshake, to an interest in the right sports, conservative politics, and understated cars. Women bankers learn not to be too "aggressive," too "masculine," or too "feminine." Too anything scares the hell out of bankers. In short, for good-looking white Protestant males of average intelligence with a low need to take risks and a high need for structured support systems, banking is a terrific fraternity. And this is exactly what *you*, an entrepreneur, have to deal with when you walk in to get money. People who spend all of their lives taking risks — like you do — scare the hell out of most bankers.

So how do we tranquilize a banker long enough to reach into his pocket?

What Turns Bankers
on — An Illustrative Tale

We have a developer, Sam, in my hometown. Sam builds shopping centers. He doesn't have an MBA; I'm not even sure he went to college; but I do know that Sam is very, very successful at what he does. A few years back Sam borrowed a pot of construction money from a New York bank to put up a big regional shopping center. The pot started at $24 million. He had flown up to New York with his plans, met with a phalanx of Brooks Brothers bankers, reviewed all his leases with them, had shown them enough figures to keep their calculators and computers humming for months, and then, since all the numbers he had shown them worked out according to their ratios, they made him the construction commitment for $24 million. Sam came home and went to work. But work went poorly: worst spring weather in a decade, they ran into rock, more bad weather, cost overruns for drainage and foundations, then a couple of major design changes, a sub went broke, and lo and behold, in a year Sam had spent the $24 million but was only 75% finished with the shopping center.

Down came the young New York bankers on Eastern Flight 361, the bankers wearing pinstripes and carrying leather attaché cases, Sam in sackcloth and ashes and carrying his hat in his hands. All the way from the airport to the job site, Sam cried mea culpa. He apologized for his miserable performance as a developer, his ignorance of modern accounting, and his letting them down so badly.

They toured the site for two hours. (Did they know a sill from a soffit?) Finally, they all sat down in Sam's office. "Fellows," he said, "I wouldn't blame you one bit if you pulled the rug out from under me right now. In fact, that's probably what you should do. I have let you down and I'm hurting for it." "Wait a minute, Mr. Sam," says they (hell, the one thing they don't want is another bankrupt shopping center to write off this year), "what would it take you to finish up — right from today?" "Well," says Sam, "it could be done for $6 million and here are the pro formas to back it up." "We'll see what we can do," they said as they trooped back on board Eastern 626 for Laguardia.

What did Sam know? First, he figured that a banker would rather make another questionable loan than precipitate a sure write-off. Second, he knew that bankers love neatly typed numbers on high-quality paper. Third, he guessed that bankers' egos respond to deferential treatment as quickly as do yours and mine.

Payoff

Armed with Sam's new pro formas, his bankers get him another $6 million. (What's another $6 million loan compared with a foreclosure — especially if you don't know a sill from a soffit?) Sam smiles and goes back to work. The bankers' brigade flies down twice more over the next twelve months, Sam bluffing through on a two-pair hand with no money on the table. And twice more the guys in the three-piece suits fold. Finally, the shopping center is finished. What a relief! The total tab is $36 million, and New York has financed the whole game. Sam has "made his," and the bankers have earned their age (in thousands) through perspicacious field work, immaculate pro formas, a perfectly documented and organized loan file, and a $36 million deed of trust on a $28 million shopping center.

What happened here? The bankers played the whole game without ever looking at the faces of the players. They went strictly by the face-up cards. (No one ever taught them differently.) Whereas they didn't understand Sam, Sam not only understood them, he also understood playing poker. Poker is not on the curriculum in our MBA program.

SHORT PRIMER ON GETTING MONEY FROM BANKERS

Levin's Second Rule: Always
Promote Competition
in the Banking Industry

Last year during a financial management seminar in Atlanta, I did a quick and dirty survey among the forty participants to see how many of them did business with more than one bank. Here are the results:

Bank with	Number responding
1 bank	11
2 banks	24
3 banks	4
4 banks	1

Let's spend a minute analyzing the results. If you go out to buy a new car and you don't get the deal you want with the first dealer, most of you would ride down the road a bit till you got one you thought reasonable. And look at it another way: if there were laws limiting the number of car dealers you were permitted to deal with to one, then you could really get screwed (just look at what's happening to the phone companies as competition comes in!).

So why did eleven out of forty, say, a quarter of those surveyed, deal exclusively with one bank? "Because, Dick, they give me everything I want." Sounds reasonable. Next question: Have they always been so generous? "Well, there have been times when they pulled in their horns and I was left a little dry." Third question: Do they make you sign personally for everything the corporation borrows? "Of course." Fourth question: When they figure out how much to lend you, do they figure your debt-to-equity ratios using historic or market value balance sheet ratios? "They take it right out of our audited books." Final question: Do you see why you need to do business with more than one bank? "Do cows give milk?"

It's not difficult to see that competition in banking like competition everywhere else usually results in better terms, lower interest rates, different views on signing personally, and a host of other potential benefits for the small-company borrower.

Look back at the survey for a moment. If you get forty smart people in a room, most of whom make money, and you find out that 72.5% of them $(24 + 4 + 1)/40$ are doing the same thing — using more than one bank in this instance — then it's fair to infer that they might be onto something good. It's a simple model, but it works: for a good piece of pie, always stop at a truck stop with a lot of cars and trucks around it. Same with a good idea — like doing business with more than one bank.

But Won't My First Banker
Get Mad?

Probably, or at least he will act mad. But Ford got mad when Carter beat him, and Carter got mad when Reagan beat him, and Reagan got mad when he didn't get an Oscar, so, don't ever worry about people getting mad, especially when you have to pay to keep them from getting mad.

Do it in an uptown style, though. Don't let them find out from someone else that you are dealing with two banks, for God's sake. They have records, and they know who's doing business with what bank, so go right in and tell them upfront. "Mike, you know you're my primary banker and I look to you as my banker in my major commercial transactions, but I have just changed my payroll account to the 32nd National Bank of Mountain View. It's not much money, but my cousin is president there, you know, and they did call on me and ask for help in getting their new bank started . . .". And so forth. Easy, painless, and lets Mike know right away that you support a competitive free enterprise banking system.

Then when your major credit line is in the bag for next year at your "primary bank," go around to the 32nd National and see if you can get some concessions there. Press for corporate loans (small ones to start with) without personal endorsement, press for slightly lower interest rates, press to use market values of your assets to figure out debt-to-equity ratios and maximum loan amounts. And if you are still paying banker 1 with compensating balances, work on that. Press them on lending you a little bit of money for longer than a year. After all, what have you got to lose? Your primary commercial financing is already taken care of, and it's like asking someone to go to bed with you. The worst that can happen is that the answer will be "no".

Caveat 1: Never press your primary banker just when you need to increase your credit line. Always get your basic credit needs lined up first before you press.

Caveat 2: Never try to press on more than two of these items at the same time. There are limits. Notice that even stick-up artists don't say, "Your money *and* your life."

Levin's Third Rule: Give Bankers
What They Need and Love

Sam won the poker game because he gave the big-city bankers what they needed, lots of nice neat clean white pro formas. Bankers thrive on numbers. If it's numbers they want, numbers they shall get. Unfortunately, however, most real cowboy capitalists are absolutely awful at working up pages and pages of pro forma balance sheets, income statements, and cash budgets. Who has time for paperwork?

If that describes you, get yourself a smart number-crunching grunt to put the figures in columns and rows. Hire an MBA who can extract pro formas from a computer *and* who understands that the game is getting money from the banks, and who doesn't confuse that game with modern financial management (which is a quite different game played largely in MBA programs).

Show up at your bank armed to the teeth. The more numbers you have crunched, the more difficult it will be for your banker to find out anything about the assumptions your number-crunching grunt used to produce all the numbers.

Always do quarterly balance sheets, P & Ls, and cash budgets. If you can get your hands on a computer program that can produce pro formas for you, you'll be golden. You can really blow their minds with ten pages of output. Remember, what your banker needs is evidence — reasonable looking numbers — to take to his or her boss who will take it to the loan committee to prove (with numbers) that you can make enough cash to pay them back. Whether your banker likes you ain't really the point, chum. He or she simply can't stand up in front of the loan committee with a pro forma you scratched out on the back of an old envelope and say, "This is a great guy who needs the money." Remember, these people are risk averse; they can find ten reasons *not* to lend you the money. You need to give them *one* good reason why they should. *Moral:* Sooooo, send your banker into the meeting armed to the teeth. Give 'em what they like best:

> columns and rows
> columns and rows
> columns and rows
> columns and rows

TRAINING YOUR BANKER
TO DO THE NEW TRICKS

B. F. Skinner Was Right: You Can
Teach Pigeons to Dance

Each of us learns by doing. Each of us has some fear the first time we do something, and each of us overcomes that fear with reinforcement in the form of a string of successes. Bankers are no exception. The first time he looks at you, he can't tell whether you're a bank robber or an honest businessperson — both tend to wear better clothes these days. After you repay the first loan ahead of time, his suspicions soften. After ten solid years in a banking relationship (read that ten years when he probably lent you about two-thirds of what you really needed), maybe he'd let you take his kid sister out. It's like old-time courting: first you hold hands, then you kiss goodnight, except that wooing a banker takes years and years — like watching a glacier race over a yard-long course. Remember as we go through the pigeon training exercise two more rules for dealing with bankers. *Levin's Rule 4:* Everything is negotiable, and I do mean everything. *Levin's Rule 5:* If you don't ask, they ain't going to offer, and you ain't going to get.

Personal Endorsements

This is the banker's little Machiavellian method of ensuring that your corporate veil is continuously pierced, at least as far as the bank's security is concerned. And all the time you thought when you started a corporation that *it* stood for its debts and that the family stood for the family's debts. Baloney. That's what they teach in the first week of a business law course. In the real world, it's called, "Lucy, will you and Charles sign here, please."

My lawyer Skip, my wife Charlotte, and I went over to Raleigh to close a permanent loan on an apartment complex we had just built. This was right after my "primary banker" Pete had pulled the rug out from under me by failing to live up to a loan commitment he had made a year previously.

Money was tight. Anyhow, I had finally found some mortgage money from a shady looking character whose lawyer showed up at the closing with a ten-page deed of trust containing clauses I had never heard of. I was strung out financially from having built the whole damn thing with my own cash, but I didn't like the terms. I sat there an hour badgering the lawyers about what this clause and that clause meant. Finally, Skip wrapped it all up very neatly for me. "Dick," he said, "the best way I can explain it to you is, if you really need the money, you and Charlotte sign right here." I signed. So did Charlotte. Skip has such a way with words.

Glacier Racing

The only way to get out of making personal endorsements is to convince your banker(s) that you are indeed credit-worthy as a *corporation,* and the best way to do that is over time. First, you take out one small loan on the credit-worthiness of the corporation alone — no personal signatures — say, just $10,000. You pay this back and the next time you ask for $25,000. It's like first you hold hands, then. . . . Remember, it's easier if you're courting more than one at the same time.

What you *don't* do is march up to numero uno and demand to be removed as personal guarantor on all your corporation's notes. That's nonsense! Bankers are risk averse, but most of them are not stupid. Move slowly and deliberately. Ask, don't demand, but ask, ask, and keep asking. You know the rule: if you don't ask, you ain't gonna get.

Crossing the Rubicon — Term

Having to pay back all the money you owe once a year is a real drag from your point of view. From the banker's perspective, it keeps his maturities under control (you know, borrow long, lend short) and leaves him with the lever to pull if your balance sheet or P & L ratios begin to go sour. In short, it absolves him from having to do any long-range planning and thereby denies you the ability to do much yourself. And that's what you call a drag in every sense of the word.

Most small corporation borrowing is for less than a year. (The exception is long-term mortgages if the real estate is held by the corporation — which generally is *not* a good idea. See Chapter 4.) I say most — remember that survey of forty people I did in Atlanta concerning how many banks they dealt with? Well, I also asked them how many had long-term debt that was not mortgage debt. Five said they did. Now five out of forty is no landslide, but it's a start.

When AT&T, IBM, and Exxon need long-term debt, they call their investment banker; when the Amalgamated Mobile Home Wheel Manufacturing Company, Inc., needs long-term debt, the banker says, "Sorry, we're just not in that business." Which is nonsense. Of course, they are in that business. What he really means is that, although he has long-term money (up to ten-year loans), you ain't gettin' any of it.

The way you train him is to get him across the Rubicon with a small loan for, say, fifteen months — anything longer than a year. It's like the old joke about making a deal with the prostitute: once you've established what she is, price is the only thing that remains to be settled. Work your banker up from fifteen months to two years, not on all your credit line, but on a small part of it. Show him or her that you are creditworthy. Creditworthy is the sacred word — do it in needlepoint and hang it in your office, because that's who bankers make loans to — "creditworthy" customers. And remember being deemed creditworthy means lots and lots of pro forma balance sheets, income statements, and cash budgets. Armed with these, your banker gets an A+ with the loan committee when he or she asks for a two-year term on your next loan.

To begin to do some really worthwhile longer-term financial planning (both for family and corporation), you have got to begin to get your name and your spouse's name off the corporate notes, and you have got to get your hands on financing that doesn't require you to reinvent the entire debt side of the balance sheet every year. Remember Skinner's pigeons, they'll do most anything for a peanut. Well, bankers love to lend money to folks who behave like the borrowers they studied back in MBA finance courses. But they go out of their gourd when you walk in late, overdrawn, with no numbers, and ask for money. *Back to Rule 3:* Give 'em what they love and need.

Figuring Debt Ratios
Using Market Values

Bankers love to cipher up their version of the maximum amount of debt your corporation can stand, read that "can pay back." Their favorite ratio here is the debt-to-equity ratio, and when it gets the tiniest bit above .4 they begin to quiver in their shoes. Listen, .4 is next to nothin'. I have this friend in Modesto, California, with a debt-to-equity ratio of 9.0! Now that's livin' high on other folks' money!

One of the problems with debt-to-equity ratios is that the real value of your assets is always carried on the balance sheet at historical cost less depreciation and not at current market value. Obviously, the "value" of your assets affects the real value of your equity. If your banker gets a fixation on using historical values to calculate debt-to-equity ratios, you are in trouble, friend. The only thing that stays at historical value is the debt! Your equity should be rising in value every single year owing to inflation and (I trust) smart purchasing. When your company is growing, you cannot afford to let your banker cut off your debt supply by acting as if your assets were worth *less* than what you paid for them twenty years ago, not with prices what they are today.

A few enlightened bankers already play the game of lending based on market value of assets, but too many of them are still wedded to the formal balance sheet — you know, the one that says "prepared in accordance with generally accepted accounting principles." Take note of what bank competition can do for you (*Levin's second rule*). If your primary banker won't recognize the true value of your assets when he or she puts together a loan package, find another banker. It don't cost a penny to shop.

With a Banker
Everything Is Negotiable

A group of us put together a real estate development in Chapel Hill years ago with $180,000 of equity and $5,400,000 of loans. Now that's leverage! (It was easier then.) The largest of our five local banks was putting up the bulk of the debt, and they went along with us (no personal signatures either). After all, we were professors and business school professors at that. Oh, and the bank's city executive was one of our former MBAs.

When we went back to the bank for money to start the golf course, he came across. When we asked for money to pay the road contractor, it was there. In 1974 the bottom fell out: our apartment developer backed out on us, interest rates went up like a rocket (you didn't think he was lending us all that money for nothing did you?), and we ran plumb out of cash.

Five of us went down to see Jim one afternoon and asked for another quarter of a million, and Jim rose to the challenge. "That's perfectly OK with the bank," he said. "We are happy to be able to help you with your plans — tell you how we'll structure it." (We all listened closely here.) "The bank will put up another quarter of a million, and you guys put up another quarter of a million, how's that?"

We went home and thought about it. We looked at our projections again, did some quick ciphering, and told Jim he owned the development. No hard feelings, we simply walked away. Putting up $180,000 of real money to take a flyer was one thing. Putting up another $250,000 (and what looked like still another $500,000 before we would see it through) was clearly different. We folded our hand.

Jim never said a word; he repossessed the project,

hired a manager, sold the lots, paid off the other creditors, and got the bank out — all in four years and with only $1,500,000 additional money put in. *Moral:* If you are holding three aces bet like hell — if you got a pair of threes and draw nothing, fold. Jim went on to become president of a bank in Ohio; we wrote off our $180,000 that year and bought some apartments.

Persistence Pays off

One of the smartest MBAs I ever had was a guy named Bill. He worked for a bank for a couple of years, then started a mortgage insurance company in 1974 and went public in the same year, no small feat given the economic climate at that time. A year into the business, Bill saw that he was not going to be able to grow and qualify to write insurance in a number of states without substantial debt financing. So he went down to the bank where he used to work and asked them for a loan of $2.5 million. Whaaat!!!

They assumed he was crazy — a twenty-eight-year-old kid, new business, no track record. Why, they had never made an equity loan of that size in the history of the damn bank (and it was a $2 billion bank by then). Well, Bill just kept asking. He was a computer nut, so he ginned up five years of projected income statements and showered those bankers with printouts — kept on and on until, lo and behold, the bank lent him $2.5 million — the largest equity loan they had *ever* made. Seek and ye shall find.

One final story about everything being negotiable. Back before the 1974 real estate recession, I borrowed some money on property. The banker gave me a choice: 10% fixed rate or prime plus 2%. Since prime was then 7% and I was farsighted enough to know absolutely for certain that it would never rise above that, I took prime plus 2%. You know the rest. Prime rose and rose and rose until I was paying 15% interest (which wouldn't have looked so bad in 1981 but was unheard of in 1974).

I really do believe that everything is negotiable with a bank, that there are no fixed rules whatever except that you have to pay the money back. So I went back to the banker and said straight up, "I'm paying too damn much interest on this note, John." He looked at me for a bit then replied, "OK, Dick, let me look over your account and I'll see what I can do." He called back the next morning to offer a fixed rate considerably lower than prime plus 2% for the remaining term (twelve years) of the note. I took it with grateful thanks. I was such a flop at interest rate forecasting I didn't want to push my luck being cute. *Moral:* If you don't ask, you won't get. Look 'em in the eye and don't blink.

OK, so much for how we look at bankers. Let's steal a leaf from their book — literally — and see how they look at us. Once more, forewarned is forearmed.

EXCERPTS FROM THE BIG BLACK BOOK OF A LARGE BANK IN YOUR NEIGHBORHOOD

How the Banker Looks at the Prospective Borrower (That's You) from Behind That Friendly Smile

SUPPORT

1. DO YOU USE A PUBLIC ACCOUNTING FIRM?

   (Bankers like Big Eight; good regional firms are also OK.) The bigger the loan you request, the more they want a full audit. Bankers don't want to get burned.

2. DO YOU HAVE THE RIGHT KIND OF ATTORNEY?

   Bankers don't want you getting sued either. Your attorney(s) should be expert in appropriate areas to you — contracts, product liability, etc.

3. DO YOU ALREADY HAVE A BANKING RELATIONSHIP?

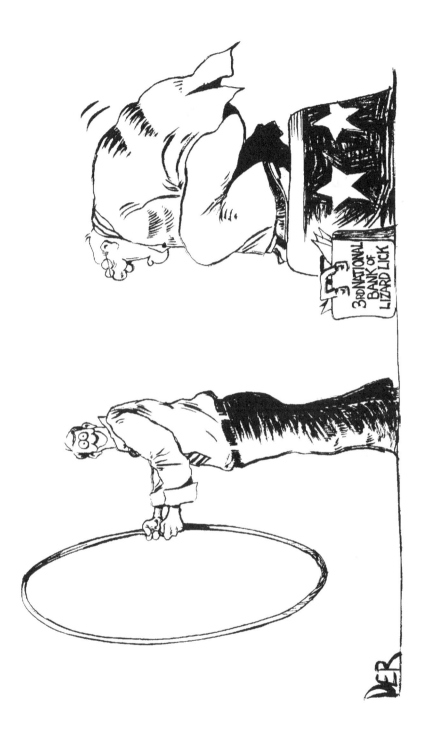

If you don't, why not? If you have — or have had — 3 or 4, why so many?

4. DO YOU CARRY ENOUGH INSURANCE?

Not just fire and casualty — but also life insurance on key people in the company. The insurer should be a familiar (big) name to the banker.

COMPARISONS

5. WHAT'S THE QUALITY AND STRENGTH OF MANAGEMENT IN YOUR COMPANY?

Do you know numbers, your niche in the industry, your competitors' strengths and weaknesses? If you drop dead at tennis this afternoon, can anyone else lead the troops? Will there be a fight for succession or an orderly transition?

6. HOW DO YOU COMPARE WITHIN YOUR INDUSTRY?

They'll *Robert Morris* you, they'll estimate your long-term viability within the industry, they'll check out the strength of your suppliers and customers.

PRO FORMAS

7. COULD YOU PROVIDE US WITH THREE PRIOR YEARS' BALANCE SHEETS AND INCOME STATEMENTS, PLEASE?

Bankers wonder if you've been around three years. They wonder about the quality of your internal accounting help. And they want those ratios revealing your liquidity, capitalization, and asset utilization.

8. COULD YOU PROVIDE US WITH A CASH BUDGET, PLEASE?

The bankers want to see your current and proposed debt maturities with cash flow to meet them.

NITTY GRITTY

9. WHY ARE YOU BORROWING?

10. WILL YOU BE A PROFITABLE CUSTOMER LONG TERM?

    Bankers will cipher up your average borrowing, relate interest rates to average borrowing, consider your compensating balance, and look for other benefits of banking with you: your personal account, spouse and kids' accounts, payroll account, trust services, account reconciliation service, lock box, and so forth. Bankers wonder: Will you grow over the long term? Will you bring in new customers?

WRAP UP: A COUPLE OF POINTS TO REMEMBER (NOT IN THE BIG BLACK BOOK)

1. Rapport is important; the banker should trust you. Have the banker out to your company to see it in person. Avoid surprising your banker if you're having trouble; let the banker hear it from you, not through the grapevine.

2. Deal with the senior loan officer, the person with the clout.

3. There has to be give and take — sometimes the bank gives up some spread, sometimes you accept a little more when the banker is in trouble. There should be more to your relationship than price; for instance, the banker should be sending you customers.

SIDE-DOOR AND BACK-DOOR
BANKING

Factoring and Such, or Would
You Step Around to the Side
Door, Please

If your statement is not too strong, chances are the bank just won't let you have seasonal credit lines, much less term loans for more than a year. Bankers tend to say things like, "Uh, Mr. Jones, given your financial strength at this time, the bank is just not able to continue a traditional commercial line relationship with you; however, you are such a valuable customer that we are going to make a special effort to take care of your working capital needs in our financing division on 8th Street." That's bankerese for "Son, lending you money on a straight commercial basis is too damn risky for us — go around to the back door and we'll lend you less for more." Now, less for more means they will take your receivables and lend you, say, 70% of them; then they may lend you 50 to 60% on your inventory (if it is not too specialized); finally they will do you this favor for about five percentage points above what you would have paid at the front door. Banditry, usury! OK, bandits, rogues, and usurers they may be, but remember what my lawyer Skip said to me, "Dick, if you want the money, just sign right here."

Factoring is not a dirty word. Tens of thousands of companies use this arrangement to obtain working capital. It costs more than traditional bank loans, yes, but if you need the money and can afford the interest rates, you take it any way you can get it!

Now You See It, Now You Don't

Things to watch out for when factoring:

1. Factoring rarely gives you the amount of money you need to grow at the rate you'd like to.

2. The high interest rates are rough unless you operate with hefty gross margins.

Suppose, for example, that the bank does lend you 70% of the face value of your accounts receivable. Then, every time you sell something to someone on credit, you run down to the back door of the bank with your invoice (sure gets you in the habit of billing early), and they put 70% of that amount in your checking account more or less. What this means is that you collect only 70% of what you sell (see, if you were rich, you'd collect 100% of what you sold — but later). The bank "keeps" the other 30%, letting you draw down only the 70% portion. Now, if your gross margin is only 20% on what you manufacture, you need 80% of your sales figure to pay for labor and materials; ergo, you have to come up with some additional bucks. Side-door banking to the rescue again — give them your inventory purchase documentation and, if you're lucky, they'll lend you 50% of that.

The arithmetic goes sorta like this. You begin the month with $1,000,000 of inventory of sheet steel on hand (which you bought with your own money — don't worry about where you got the money: marry rich, rob a bank, start a new religion, but remember Uncle Lou's dictum — it takes money to make money). Then, you pay $1,000,000 for the labor to make mobile home wheels this month and $250,000 for light bills, lawyers' bills, accountants' bills, telephone bills, and everything else that will be shut off if you don't pay! Then you use all these inputs (as my colleagues are fond of saying) totaling $2,250,000 to manufacture mobile home wheels, which you sell on credit for $2,700,000, which is a 20% markup on cost — take your $2,700,000 worth of invoices around to the side door of the bank where they lend you 70% of that or $1,890,000. While you're there, you show them your inventory receipts for $1,000,000 (paid for with your own mysterious money source) on which they lend you 50% or another $500,000.

So this trip to the side door nets you $1,890,000

plus $500,000 for a grand total of $2,390,000 to take home in your satchel. But you've spent this month $1,000,000 for labor, $1,000,000 for inventory, and $250,000 for "disconnectable overhead," and your inventory is gone! Your trip to the bank nets you $2,390,000 − $2,250,000 = $140,000. Well, at least you end the month with a positive cash balance. Wait, there is more — there's interest and next month.

First, the side-door boys clip you 25% interest, which comes to about $50,000, which leaves you with $90,000. So you go home and buy $90,000 of inventory with your own money, and having no cash left, you ask your workers to wait till the end of the month to get paid. Then under the fairness doctrine you ask all the purveyors of "disconnectable overhead" to wait till the end of the month too . . . wait . . . wait . . . this is nonsense!

Right, but I said it ten pages ago. If you don't have some money to begin with, and if your gross margin isn't pretty high, it's damn difficult to live and prosper with the boys at the side door. It's like the story of the frog who tumbles down the well and who falls back three feet every time he jumps up two feet — a hell of a lot of good exercise but he dies just the same. Take heart, if interest rates on your factored receivables and inventory fell to 20%, then you would have $100,000 to start the next month with! Better to start a new religion! Or get your money from the boys in black shirts and white ties. Their rates are only about 5% — a week, that is.

Who Finances the Real Cowboys?
Banks?

Ha, now there's a myth for you! Remember, banks just are not in the business of taking risks, especially not financing new ventures, like your car that runs on water. If bankers took big risks, they'd demand equally big rewards, like a piece of the action. But big-time risk taking is a completely different business, and banks are just not geared philosophically to handle entrepreneurs, particularly those who need to grow fast! Venture capital comes from venture capitalists, who are another breed. They include

1. Traditional partnerships often established by wealthy families to manage aggressively a portion of their funds by investing in small companies.
2. Professionally managed pools of money made up of institutional money and managed like family partnerships.
3. Investment banking firms (I mentioned the fearless one or two out of every MBA class that go for the moon), which usually trade in more established securities but which occasionally form investor syndicates for venture proposals.
4. Insurance companies that will sometimes advance venture capital in exchange for a part of the equity in smaller companies.
5. Manufacturing companies that sometimes look on small-company venture investments as a way to supplement their own R & D operations.
6. SBICs and MESBICs — small business investment companies and minority enterprise small business investment companies chartered by the federal government under very favorable terms expressly for the purpose of providing venture capital.

But What's the Difference, Coach?

Banks look at a company's immediate future, but they are more heavily influenced by a company's past history. Venture capital firms look to the long run because most of their clients have no history! Banks are creditors; they are interested only in assurances that the sale of your products can generate cash to pay them back. Venture capital firms are equity providers (in the guise of loans, however); they invest for capital gains, not for interest income. Most venture capital loans are unprotected in the event of failure. Traditional debt-equity risk advantages don't hold water in the venture capital business. When the ship goes down, generally *all* the capital is lost. Hence, debt holders are really not that much better off than equity providers.

Since the lion's share of a company's success accrues to the equity providers, venture capitalists have little or no incentive to provide debt capital alone.

What Are the Rules on Raising
Venture Capital?

In point of fact, there ain't any. You get it any way you can! Here's a quick and dirty checklist of things you may forget in the bedlam of producing your car that runs on water:

1. Bring in stockholders whose loyalty counts when you organize; get people who have leverage with the banks. If they won't put up money, get them to cosign notes or intercede for you with their influential bank friends.
2. Preparing financial pro formas for new ventures is like sewer line contracting. You are bound to hit rock if you dig long enough, so make plans for rock — read that *financial contingencies.*
3. Lease and rent everything you can; don't confuse saving pennies with running out of dollars.
4. If you have to buy anything, buy general-purpose assets to generate maximum resale value if you go belly up.
5. Remember, the more capital you have to raise now, the more of the equity in the company you will have to give away to get it — and the smaller your pot of gold will be later.
6. Consider the "second-man-through" approach — picking up a bankrupt company or a sinking enterprise at a fire sale.
7. Don't be afraid to ask anybody for money. Remember my friend Bernice who used three different accountants to make loan applications to nine different banks, all of which failed except the last one, which lent him what he needed to get well financially in his business.

"Supermoney": High Times
in the '60s

Way back in the 1960s, a friend and I organized a small regional management consulting company. Things went well, and folks were extra nice to us, and in a couple of years we were billing nearly a third of a million dollars and netting nearly a hundred thousand. We were also working our asses off. As we looked around us we saw that everybody who was anybody was "going public" in those years, folks with nothing to sell but smoke, and here we had real dollars, a real office, real employees, and real customers. Well, we decided we should go public too — talk about chutzpah. So he and I took Eastern Flight 584 to Laguardia early one morning and made the rounds of the firms who were interested in "nothing" companies like ours. These firms were known affectionately at that time as "the whores of Wall Street." Well that day we met four whores who gave us great encouragement. About 2 P.M., we were in the fourth whore's office. He was visibly impressed with our earnings to the point of his mouth watering, and he wanted to do a deal with us. We, being a couple of hick professors from North Carolina, wanted some assurance that he knew his business. Brashly we asked if he had ever done any deals like this before. "What do you mean," he shouted as he jumped up from behind his desk, strode across the room, and threw open an eight-foot-wide floor-to ceiling closet full of prospectuses. "What do you mean, have I done many deals like this? I have done 500 pounds of deals like this!" He was so enamored of our profits and the times were so wild that he said sure he could take us public if we'd just delay our plane a couple of hours. This frankly scared the hell out of us hicks, and we left New York on schedule.

"Supermoney" — *Reprise*

A couple of months later we did go public by buying a shell corporation and merging our profitable corporation into it. I'll never forget it if I live to be a thousand. I was lying in the hospital just out of surgery when the phone rang. It was our market maker in New York who announced that our stock had begun trading that morning. It was quoted in the over-the-counter pink sheets at $.125 bid, $.25 asked — big financial dealers we were!

Well, we kept on selling consulting and we kept on hiring folks, and the stock rose in a year to $2.25 bid and $2.75 asked. Now, I was raised poor — depression kid,

$2.00 used bicycle, hand-me-down clothes from older brother Bob, the whole bit. So I decided to leave a little bit of the future for the rest of the world and get the hell out of this business. Sadly I discovered that my enormous pile of stock was "lettered," not freely tradable! What I thought was a more than $2 million net worth was a pile of paper with a red legend on the margin.

To make a long story short, during the next six months I discovered the market in lettered stock — $.15 on the dollar, trade it for what you can get, six shares for the price of one, sell it to the other stockholders and take notes — the whole damned expensive route of converting paper to money.

Well, as they say in North Carolina, I got shed of all of it. Traded most of it for apartment houses. Didn't come out a millionaire, but didn't come out as broke as I went in or as poor as I was born. Had a hell of a lot of fun, and learned a lot about 1960s "supermoney."

Nothing would surprise me, but I believe those crazy days of wild money are gone for good. The financial markets are back to rewarding buy low, sell high, collect early, and pay late. And if you don't earn $500,000 after taxes in a hot-item business, forget it. Now, if that describes your business plan for the car that runs on water, I think I could put you in touch with a couple of people in New York . . . .

FOUR

How to Put Money and Other Things in Your Organization the Right Way

Corporation: An artificial
person . . . regarded in the law as
having a personality and existence
distinct from that of its several
members . . . .

– Black's Law
Dictionary

The law of this land gives certain advantages to corporations, principally two. (1) As a stockholder you can't be
sued for corporation debts — beyond the value of your
stock, that is — and (2) the corporate form of organization
permits certain tax actions of great benefit to stockholders, not only at the time the corporation is organized but
also during its operation and even when it is liquidated.
Now, as it says in the Old Testament, there's no free lunch
in this world or the next. What that means, if you don't
follow the rules for corporations and their controlling
stockholders, is (1) you will miss many of the potential tax
advantages of having a corporation (or corporations) in
the family, and (2) you may also forgo the legal protection
of the corporate form of organization. This chapter is a
short primer on how to play the corporate/family game so
you don't lose anything — protection or benefits.

THEY CAN'T SUE ME —
I'M INCORPORATED

What the Law Says

If you run your rocket fuels corporation by the book and if
one of your corporation test rockets goes amiss, flies right
into downtown Topeka, Kansas, and wipes out everything
from the main fire station to the new elementary school,
the most you can lose is what's in your corporation. That
was one of the major reasons you elected the corporate
form of organization, remember? To gain protection in
the form of limited liability. Right!

If you play by the rules, limited liability means that the court can't get at your personal goodies owned outside the corporation, for instance, your condominiums in Hilton Head and Vail, your 602-P Turbo Pressurized Aerostar, your Maserati, your investment portfolio, or your 9,000-square-foot principal residence. All of what you own personally is immune from the bad fortune of your corporation, provided, of course, that you do play by the rules. The rules are not complicated . . .

First Commandment: Thou shalt not be guilty of gross negligence. Look, if you fire up your corporation's rocket, point it at downtown Topeka, and light the fuse, then they will not only take everything in your corporation but they will also take the house, cars, plane, condo, and anything else you have, plus put you away at the funny farm for years. Or, if the rocket guidance system was known to be unreliable — one almost hit Omaha last week — but you never did anything about it, well goodbye Maserati, goodbye Aerostar, and maybe someone will send you a nice picture postcard of Vail to brighten up your 200-square-foot cell in your new principal residence. If you, the management, behave like a model corporate citizen (keep those guidance systems in good repair and only point your rockets down the corporation rocket range), then the misfortunes of your corporation will most likely be settled with corporate assets and not with your private wealth.

Second Commandment: Thou shalt not "mix" your corporate financial life with your private financial life. The two must be kept scrupulously separate. Otherwise, any Tom, Dick, or Harry (and there are IRS agents by those names) with claims against your corporation may conclude that the artificial person bears a striking resemblance to you, when it puts *its* hand in your pocket (purse) and pulls out *your* money. So these are the commandments, all two of them.

In exchange for two very straightforward vows (sanity and separateness), you get the advantage of all the corporate legal and tax goodies. What a deal!

Do as I Say, Not as I Do, or What
Folks Often Do

The rocket fuels business was hectic about five years ago
when you had $150 in the bank, a lot of hope, and no
customers for your unproven product. Airplanes, Aspen,
foreign cars, condos — all these were far from your mind
as you watched the pile of bills grow and answered irate
phone calls from your creditors. In a continuing crisis,
your corporate financial "system" becomes sort of like
Sam the fishman's cigar-box cash system: when you need
money, you dig in your "personal" pocket and come up
with a thousand bucks, which you then put in the corporate bank account without a note from the corporation,
without a document, without anything. Then a month
later, you sell some of the stuff you're making and forget-
fully deposit the $2,000 check in your personal bank ac-
count. A week after that, you remember that the corporation owes you $1,000, so you write yourself a check on the
corporation for your thousand bucks. This nice, easy,
informal, no-hassle financing system continues for five
years, money passing back and forth, back and forth, no
notes, no minute books, no records, no nothin'.

Time goes on. The rocket fuels business prospers,
and still you trade dollars. Now the numbers on the balance sheet have more zeros after them than they used to,
but then, so do the banknotes in your personal pocket.
Nowadays you cash in a $10,000 personal CD and put it in
the business (just for a week till the California customer
sends the check, you say to your bookkeeper). One month
you're a bit short for payroll, so you take out a $50,000
mortgage on your new house and put the money in the
business — no need to sign a note, you tell the bookkeeper
again, the money will be paid back in less than thirty days.
And, by God, it is. Your big customer in North Africa sends
you $50,000, but the check is made payable to you. Well, of
course you don't send it all the way back — hell, the government may have changed again — no, you endorse it to
your bank to pay off the note on your house. So it goes for
five years, transaction after transaction, your own version

of a corporate-personal shell game. Until 3 o'clock this afternoon when, that's right, the rocket wipes out downtown Topeka. "Oh Lord, don't even let them *think* that artificial person is me!"

Enter the Law
in a Three-Piece Suit

Armed with a court order, the young lawyer spends two weeks in your office, and he's been primed by his old MBA program buddy, now a successful CPA in Topeka (with an office, it happens, only two blocks from the crater you made). He's there to "pierce the corporate veil." Sounds nasty, doesn't it. Means he wants to stick his hands in the corporate pocket and see if he jingles *your* change. That is, he's looking for conclusive evidence that you have not operated your corporation as a separate legal entity but rather as an extension of your personal affairs. What evidence? Let's see it! Well, how about all those checks that banks routinely microfilm these days? That should give them a start.

When you get to court, you see that the judge is about thirty-two years old, has a beard, and looks suspiciously like one of the kids who demonstrated in front of your plant a few years back when you started making rocket fuels for Third World customers. "Damn! Where's my veil when I need it most? Hey, you can't take my Maserati! I'll escape in my Aerostar, leave me alone!"

Get the point? If you've been less than a paragon of financial and legal virtue in separating your corporate and family affairs, spend a little time tonight vowing to straighten things out — *before* your rocket hits Topeka.

> BUT I DO HAVE THEM ALL
> STRAIGHT

Bully for You and Your Lawyers

So you've lived a model life and the most detailed scrutiny of your personal and corporate books cannot turn up one shred of evidence that you have commingled those affairs.

No one jingles the change in your pockets but you. Good for you, the folks in Topeka can't sue you and collect. But you can still lose the war! That's right, even if you do everything right legally, you can still screw up royally. Watch!

A Better Mousetrap,
but Someone Else Built It

The years go by, you become the rocket fuels king of the whole world. You lead a very frugal personal life — no cars, no plane, no condo, no 9,000-square-foot residence. Just work and money, work and money. And you really do pile it up! You amass a $40 million fortune, all retained inside the corporation, all owned by the corporation, and all of it invested in the form of plant, equipment, and current assets necessary to manufacture rocket fuels.

Then one day the government discovers a new laser, you know, one that bends around corners, goes through culverts, is trained to miss little kids and kill all the bad guys, one that doesn't eat much or join unions, and one that just plain beats the livin' hell out of any rocket fuel you have. Damn!

2 − 2 = 0

Here you are now, every damn dime you own inside the corporation, invested in a product that just became obsolete. Libya and every other country that buys from you immediately cancels outstanding orders, your stock goes straight to hell, the plant and equipment is worthless because nobody in the whole world wants rocket fuel any more. And there you sit, legal as a judge, but with a classic Business Policy 101 single-purpose business strategy and no customers. Light dawns? So *that's* why oil companies buy coal companies, and newspapers buy TV stations, and . . . .

Reprise

So you see, chum, it's not only necessary to watch your financial and legal Ps and Qs so that the folks in Topeka can't get your ass, it's also absolutely essential to have what I call a proper inside-outside split of the wealth. You generally cannot afford to wind up with all your hard-earned wealth locked up inside the corporation. In a later chapter, we'll tell you some ways to get the wealth you've created out of the corporation with a minimum tax bite, but that's tax strategy. Here, we're preaching about corporate strategy — and the misfortune of having a product that no one wants. When that happens to you, a creative tax strategy is number 11 on a list of three things you ought to be worrying about. So, in the final analysis, remember these three commandments:

1. Avoid gross negligence.
2. Keep your corporation's financial affairs completely separate from your family's financial affairs.
3. Decide on an appropriate split of your wealth (some inside and some outside the corporation) and work toward attaining that goal.

The last time I surveyed friends and clients of mine about their inside-outside split, it turned out that the average split was about two-thirds outside of the corporation. Now these are smaller companies (annual sales from about $3 million to $45 million), and my survey doesn't represent a statistically significant sampling of the population. But I do put credence in the judgment of a lot of smart business folks who have thought about the inside-outside split issue for years and have somehow come to two-thirds outside conclusion. Sure, it's nice to have the company support some of your luxuries, like the beach and mountain houses, the jet, and the Maserati. After all, it's *your* overhead either way, and if you can expense some of the personal stuff, that's the better way, right?

Well, maybe the proper inside-outside split for you depends on (1) how much you love and would miss your toys if they were suddenly taken away and (2) the volatility of the product you sell — how likely it is to dry up, or blow up in your face, taking your wealth with it.

PUTTING MONEY
IN THE CORPORATION

Stock vs. Loans —
A Cautionary Tale

Putting your money in a corporation, either in the beginning or farther on down the road, is a crucial decision. Obviously, if you don't put some money in to start, it's hard as hell to do any business on no money. So your lawyer says to you, "George, suppose you put in a thousand dollars to start, and we'll issue you stock in exchange for that." Nothing wrong so far — a thousand dollars is little enough capital for any self-respecting corporation. Now time goes on, the financing needs of the company increase, and you keep putting in more of your money and taking more stock for it. The profits continue to increase, the retained earnings look good, and your hoard of stock certificates in the safe deposit box is getting so fat you're going to need the next size larger box very soon. You've paid a penny or two in dividends a couple of times, so there are even a few bucks you've managed to get outside of the corporation (unfortunately, out of after-tax profits, but I don't want you to think I'm carping).

Well, twenty years go by and the owners' equity account is upwards of $8,000,000—"Great heavens, I had no idea we were worth that much! Whoopee, time to take some of that out and have some fun!" Whoa, cowboy. Your trouble's just beginning. How do you get money out of a corporation without getting killed on the taxes if you already are paying yourself a reasonable salary and bonus? Answer: you don't! "Say it ain't so, coach!" Wish I could, but it's so! "You mean the only way I can get that money out now is to pay it out in dividends? My God, in my tax bracket, the income tax on it will take at least half." You got it. "There *must* be some other way." Oh, there is, there is. You can liquidate the corporation and if your horoscope is right, you can get somewhat more favorable tax treatment of the proceeds. "But, damn, it is making money now, and I don't want to liquidate it . . . and my kids aren't old enough to take over . . . and I am not ready to retire, and, dammit, a third of that is money I put in myself to grow!" Sorry, should have thought of that when you were putting all that money in the company. "Thanks a lot."

A Better Way, or the Moral of the Cautionary Tale

Next time you're about to put money (or anything of value for that matter) into your corporation, consider *lending* it to the corporation, not giving it in exchange for stock. On a loan, if and when you want to get the money out again, just reach in there and take it out. There is no one to stop you — you own the whole damn thing anyhow. And there is no tax whatsoever; a loan is a loan. "But what if the company goes down the tubes and I'm sitting there holding a note for a million bucks? Wouldn't it be better to have stock to back my claim?" Friend, let's be honest about small corporations. When they go down the tubes, there ain't even enough most times to pay the bank and the creditors, let alone leave anything for the stockholders. When they go down, they generally go all the way.

So be smart. When you have to add capital to the company, add it, but don't call it equity capital, call it loans. It's your money anyhow, wherever it is. Why not put it under current liabilities where you can get it out in ten minutes tax free, rather than down in the equity section where you have to lie, cheat, and steal to get it out, and get killed with taxes in the bargain. Doesn't matter a damn how long that loan will be in there either. If you intend to leave it in longer than a year, take notes for it just like you would if you intended for it to stay in a month. Pay yourself interest too. That's a good way to get a few bucks out of the corporation — before taxes too!*

Caveat: As always, bring your tax lawyer or accountant in at the beginning, *before* you make a loan to your company in lieu of adding equity. All actions involving closely held companies are subject to close scrutiny by the IRS, which will look beyond the form to the substance of an act. If the IRS think they have a case, they can say that your "loan" is equity. And equity, if it comes back out of the company, comes out as a dividend. Taxed to the max, of course. *Moral:* Don't get caught wearing a flimsy veil — consult your tax professional.

If you Must Take Stock,
Take 1244

Section 1244 of the Internal Revenue Code contains a few goodies for folks like you and me, namely, 1244 stock. Now 1244 stock is printed on the same paper as "regular" stock, the certificates are the same size, and you can sell it just like regular stock, and you can lose your pants in a corporation that has issued 1244 stock just as fast as you can lose them in any other corporation. But when and if you lose your pants in a corporation that has issued 1244 stock instead of ordinary stock, better things tend to happen to what, if anything, is left of your hindparts. Witness: the loss on the stock if your corporation goes belly up is fully deductible from ordinary income as an ordinary loss. This treatment is an awful lot better than a capital loss with limits on the annual deduction if you don't happen to have an offsetting capital gain. Now that's one the Lord giveth. I mean, who wants to prolong the agony of losing by carrying it forward from here to eternity — 1244 lets you wallop your tax return with the whole loss and get on with your life. Let's hear it for 1244!

No free Big Macs in America. Here are a few rules that govern the issuance of 1244 stock as of this writing.

1. For any taxable year, the aggregate loss cannot exceed $50,000 on a single return or $100,000 on a joint return, whether the stock is owned by one or both spouses.

2. Any loss more than $50,000 (single return) or $100,000 (joint return) is treated as a capital loss and can be carried forward if not used up.

3. Your claimed loss cannot be more than the money or property you gave in exchange for the stock.

4. You must be the original holder of that stock, either directly or through a partnership. If you sell it, the buyer cannot claim 1244 treatment in the event of loss.

5. Corporations, trusts, and estates cannot claim 1244 treatment for stock they hold. Only individuals and partnerships qualify for 1244 goodies.

6. The stock must be common stock issued by a domestic corporation.

7. When you issue 1244 stock, you cannot have any other kind of prior stock offer outstanding.

8. You must issue the stock for money or property, not other stock or securities. (You may issue stock for cancellation of debt, *unless* debt is either evidenced by security or arose from services.)

9. The issuing corporation must be a small business corporation (lets most of us in — pretty loose definition) and must be an active business, not a corporation in business to invest in other companies. Also, for five years before loss, the corporation must have over 50% gross receipts from other than "passive" sources.

10. The aggregate amount of money and other property received for stock must not exceed $1,000,000.

Does that look like a formidable list? It really isn't. Most new corporations would just about qualify on all ten requirements, without the owners even thinking about it. In this instance, the Lord giveth because He in His wisdom wants to promote actively the funneling of equity capital into small corporations. And there are few incentives that surpass an attractive tax angle. It's sugar on the pill — sure, a new venture is risky — but if it goes down the tubes, you can take it off your taxes that year as an ordinary loss. (The write-off is subject to limitations, but they are generous ones compared with those for deducting capital losses.)

Directions for Best Use

If you are thinking about merging one corporation with another and one has 1244 stock, merge the one that doesn't into the one that does, so you will qualify for favorable tax treatment if the merged corporation fails later.

When you want to raise capital by issuing stock, issue 1244 stock. It is more attractive to the high-roller contributors of capital — lets them get a more favorable tax treatment if *you* go broke.

If you have a partnership you are thinking about incorporating, liquidate the partnership, distribute all the assets to the partners, and then let them transfer the

assets to the corporation in exchange for 1244 stock. If you forget to follow this sequence and you transfer the partnership assets directly to the new corporation, you still won't pay any tax (both are tax-free transactions), but neither will the corporation qualify for 1244 stock. Remember, the partners must be the *original* persons to whom the stock was issued for it to qualify under Section 1244.

If you want to be careful and document all this properly, write it up and put it in the corporate minute books. And if you are the overcautious type, print in large red letters on the side of each stock certificate — "issued under Section 1244 of the Internal Revenue Code."

CORPORATIONS, FAMILIES, AND
REAL ESTATE

The Gospel According to Dick

I tend to deal in absolutes. My absolutes change over time, but while I ascribe to them, they are absolute. My longest-running absolute is that corporations should never own real estate. That absolute has stayed with me for twenty years now and shows no signs of diminishing in vitality. There is absolutely no sane reason for your corporation to own real estate. If it does, that's dumb — there is just no nice way to say it — it's just dumb for your corporation to own real estate. OK, so I'll admit to three possible exceptions to my absolute:

1. Your corporation needs a building and the stockholders do not have the financial resources to buy it personally. The corporation, on the other hand, can afford it. For the corporation to buy it is then the *only* way it will get the building it needs to conduct its business effectively.

2. Your corporation buys a building to use up some of its retained earnings thereby avoiding a penurious tax on these earnings. (We will treat in detail methods to avoid this tax in Chapter 8.)

3. The real estate has been in the corporation for some time, and the attribution rules under Section 1239 of the code prevent you from selling it to yourself. (Section 1239 has lots and lots of nice little rules about selling and buying property between you and your own controlled corporation.)

If it ain't one of these three reasons, then having real estate in a corporation is just _____ (fill in the blank — any synonym for dumb).

How Did All This Money
Get in There?

It all began, you remember, back in 1954 in the lawyer's office when you got together to incorporate the business, you, Louise, and the lawyer. You had $10,000 and Louise had $5,000, and the both of you owned this building in which you were manufacturing house trailer wheels. (That was before they started calling them mobile homes.)

LAWYER: *George, why don't we put the whole thing in one corporation. It's so much easier to keep track of that way, and we can do the whole thing with one set of books.*
LOUISE: *We'll think it over.*
GEORGE: *Whatever you say, Esquire.*
LOUISE: *George, you're always in such a rush.*

Now that's a dumb lawyer for ya! You need to hunt him up and shoot him, just like Shakespeare said in *Henry VI,* Part II: "The first thing we do, let's kill all the lawyers." Well, years and years have gone by and the building is *still* in the corporation. Funny thing, though, the city has grown up around that lot and building, and your real estate friend mentioned the other day that he thought you could get $1,500,000 for it. Now look at this diagram and see how your building has produced equity over time against which you can borrow — *tax free,* that is.

Growth of Equity Over Time in a Building

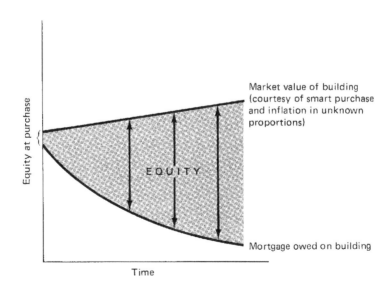

Market value of building (courtesy of smart purchase and inflation in unknown proportions)

EQUITY

Equity at purchase

Mortgage owed on building

Time

Nice work, but how in the hell are you going to get the million and a half out of the corporation without paying it out in dividends if you sell the building? Oh, forgot about that, didn't you. Too late now. All you can do is hunt up the lawyer and shoot him.

*Stuff It, Levin, I Didn't Want
to Sell It Anyway*

Saving it for the kids! Still a lousy deal. (Still shoot the lawyer.) As the building appreciates in value, the corporation can go borrow against it again and again. That's lovely if you want to keep the loan proceeds *inside* the corporation, but if you want to get them outside, it's miserable. You have to do it by paying dividends — which is what you do in a small corporation when you run out of your last sane idea. But if the *family* owned the building, you could refinance it, take the loan proceeds, and do with them whatever you want, without paying a cent of taxes to anyone.

Profits and Losses Produced by a Commercial Building

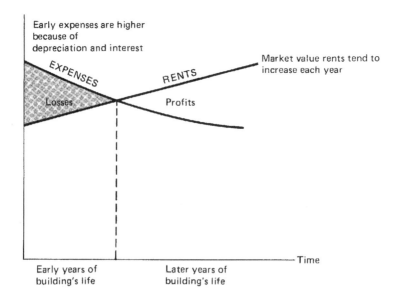

86

*So What? I Don't Want
to Mortgage It Either!*

I still recommend you shoot the lawyer who put the building in the corporation for you, because in all likelihood he screwed you out of the tax benefits you could have had. But this time, I'll need a diagram to show you why I think this way. Above is a diagram of your building over ten years of its life showing the profits and losses it will incur.

And now here's the chronological and economic line-up of your family:

Person	Age	Approximate Federal Tax Bracket
You	51	50%
Louise	50	50
Daughter #1	16	20
Son #1	13	12
Son #2	10	12
Daughter #2	8	12
Your father	74	25
Louise's mother	68	20

You are responsible for the economic welfare of this whole damn platoon, and being economically responsible includes seeing to it that the family (in the aggregate) doesn't pay more tax than it is legally liable for. Now, match the tax bracket of each family member against the last diagram showing the profit and loss produced by your building. You and Louise need losses because you're already getting soaked for taxes. The kids and your living parents can stand income (profits) because their tax brackets are low. And with the building owned by the corporation, there's not a damn thing you can do to give you and Louise what you need and the kids and parents what they need.

Suppose My Lawyer Had Known?

Ah, reminds me of what my father Meyer used to say: "If a frog had longer legs, he wouldn't bump his ass each time he jumped." But suppose, just suppose for a minute, that you had set up a family real estate partnership, with everybody in the family included in it for some share in the beginning — you and Louise with the lion's share, the living parents with a smaller share, and the children with even smaller shares. If you had done it that way — and a smart tax lawyer would have known exactly what to do, but that $30-an-hour, room-temperature I.Q. twit you use didn't — it would have looked something like this originally.

Shares in the Family Pile

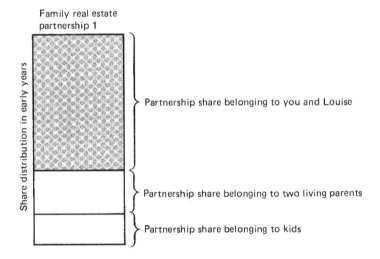

Don't worry about how all these retired or unemployed school-aged family members can afford to buy shares in family real estate partnership 1. Since the building was likely mortgaged when you bought it, equity was small and small pieces of small equity can be gifted using your annual tax-free gift allowance. Besides, your dad and Louise's mother have a few bucks anyway, and I hope you have had your kids on the corporation payroll since they were old enough to get a social security card.

What Now, Coach?

OK, so if family real estate partnership 1 had bought the building originally and had rented it to the corporation, then during the early years when the building (and, therefore, the partnership) lost money due to depreciation* and interest, you and Louise could have taken those partnership losses and deducted them from your other income (which I assume is plenty if you make mobile home wheels), saving you 50 cents on every dollar. So could your parents and the kids, but losses to them are not worth nearly as much as they are to you and Louise.

In a few years, after you have raised rents in line with the local market, the building begins to turn a profit. Now if there's anything you and Louise don't need it's profit, so each year you give additional partnership shares to the kids (and to your living parents if you like), until after five or so years they practically own the partnership, which owns the building. Then the partnership begins to look like this:

Shares in the Family Pile a Few Years Later

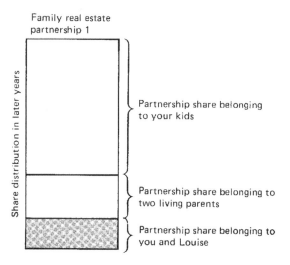

Most of the profits go to your kids who pay taxes at low rates; the next largest share of the profits goes to your living parents whose incomes are probably fixed and who

---

*Under ACRS (Accelerated Cost Recovery Schedule), if *nonresidential* real property gets accelerated depreciation treatment, gain is recaptured as ordinary income to the extent of *all* the depreciation taken. (Under old law, only the "excess" of accelerated over straight line was recaptured.) *Therefore, accelerated depreciation may not be as popular under ACRS for real property.* (Hooray! Apartment houses are still OK!)

pay taxes at only slightly higher rates. And the smallest share of the partnership profits goes to you and Louise who still get killed with taxes. (See how elegantly it all works out if you stay away from twits who tell you just to put it all in a corporation!) You let the high-bracket tax-payers take the losses in the early years, you let the low-bracket taxpayers take the profit in the later years, and the changeover is accomplished with tax-free gifts of shares. And when you get about ten years down the road, you can refinance the whole damn building and split the money among the partners with not a cent of taxes being paid. Short of a repeal of the personal income tax, it's hard to do much better.

Caveats — Just a Few

Don't try to keep the books on this partnership at the corporate office — that is a no-no. Get a *smart* impoverished young lawyer (no twits) to set the whole thing up for you and keep the books. The charges are slight, and it looks good in a tax audit. Don't try to put more than one building in a partnership; it is usually not a good idea from a tax standpoint. Tax rates change, ages of the family change, personal needs change, real estate values change, and yes, families even fall in and out of love and trust with one another over time. So, when you need a new building for the mobile home wheel plant, set up a new partnership. Use grandchildren, cousins, anybody you want, put the new building in the partnership name and rent it to the corporation, but never, never put real estate in a corporation. Meet once a year with your lawyer, review the tax situations of the family members, and adjust the shares each owns in each family partnership so that the aggregate tax paid is minimum. And you can tell the whole world what you are doing — shout it to the four winds, buy TV time — but they can't touch you, much less send you to Montgomery for tax evasion. It's all quite legal, not to mention smart.

Review: Pay Close Attention, We
May Ask Questions Later

Let's wrap up this section with a quick review of the reasons why family partnership ownership of real estate needed by corporations is to be preferred:

1. The losses from the building in the early years can be deducted from the income of the higher-tax-bracket partnership members.
2. The profits from the building in later years can be taken as income by the lower-bracket-partnership taxpayers.
3. Equity produced by perspicacious purchase of the building and inflation in its market value can be borrowed against, and this money used by the family partnership members without paying any tax.
4. Appreciation of the asset's value is retained for the family instead of the corporation.
5. This enables family business owners to pursue an appropriate inside-outside wealth location strategy.
6. The family members who bought the building and are leasing it to their corporation can include the value of the land in the lease rent. This effectively lets the corporation expense land values in its rents — something it couldn't do if it owned the real estate.
7. Setting up family partnerships helps to keep young impoverished lawyers off the streets.
8. If the corporation is unfortunate enough to have real estate inside it, it can always sell this to a family partnership (at market value, please) and lease it back. It can pay its capital gains tax on the installment basis and deduct its lease rent. This is nice from both a tax and cash flow standpoint.

FAMILY LEASING COMPANIES
ARE GREAT, TOO

Sorta the Same Thing, but Maybe
a Little Better

Forming family partnerships for the purpose of leasing vehicles and machinery to a corporation controlled by the family is just about the same thing as the family real estate partnerships we just discussed. It is quite easy to do (remember the young, impoverished lawyer routine, here); it has the same kinds of tax *avoidance* (that's the good word — the bad one is *evasion*) advantages; and since the equipment and vehicles a corporation needs represent many more *units* than the number of buildings it needs, the possibilities for creative tax sheltering are even better than with the real estate partnerships. There is no question that, when a family member or family partnership is the lessor, this provides a great way to divide up family income into piles that get slapped with lower tax rates.

But Is There Anything I Need
to Watch, Coach?

Ah yes, the Lord taketh away a little here too, but not much. Here's a short list of the "taketh aways":

1. Don't try to be too cute with options to buy at the end of a lease. Writing in nonsense like "lessee can purchase building at end of lease for $1" is exactly that, nonsense. Nobody can purchase anything under the tax laws for anything but fair market value without running afoul of the Feds. And don't forget that options to buy in general are danger signals to Feds that you are trying a cute end run. They can overturn your carefully drawn lease and call it a disguised purchase.

2. Writing in renewal options at excessively high (nonmarket value) rents is another easily discovered and just as easily overturned dumb thing to do. Any first-year IRS field auditor knows that things like this are attempts to get more money out of a corporation without paying tax on dividends, so be smart, don't try it. Rent your vehicles and equipment to the corporation at market rates.

3. Leases between family members (your corporation and your family) will hold up only if rental rates and lease terms are reasonable — where the best definition of reasonable is "approximate current market conditions" — so that, if you are getting into leasing a hell of a lot of equipment and vehicles to your corporation, spend a few bucks, get a well-known, qualified appraiser and let him or her set the prices and terms. It may save you a bundle — money *and* aggravation.

4. Don't forget that leasing trucks may involve a somewhat higher risk than leasing a building, or even machinery *in* that building. The building is not likely to fall down and kill lots of folks, whereas the truck always has the potential for causing great bodily harm, as they are fond of saying in insurance policies. This fact should not deter you from starting a family leasing operation, but it should focus your attention on the risk potential and the proper insurance remedies for situations like this.

Okay, that's it. You're incorporated with 1244 stock, and your big pile of assets is really a lot of little piles, family owned. Wonderful. Now turn the page and let's find out. . . .

FIVE

How're We Doing, Coach? Analyzing What's Right and Wrong with Your Business

> *There was a young man named West*
> *By comparisons so rudely obsessed*
> *That he, post-coital*
> *Would delightedly chortle,*
> *"Ah, that was good – no, better – the*
> *best!*

> – *Anonymous*

Everybody compares! Weekend duffers flailing away at golf balls become Nicklaus, Watson, and Lopez-Melton. Hot kids on local courts secretly serve aces past McEnroe or Austin. What struggling business owner up to his ears in bills, hopes, and promises doesn't look with yearning rivalry at the 25% after-tax return on equity earned by some of his or her high-flying competitors? It's the way of the world. Flat-chested preteens stare with wonder and envy at their buxom older sisters, and little boys who sidle up to their first public urinal glance around at the standards in evidence. And everybody knows what wins it all in their game: straight A's in school, a zero handicap on the course, top seed in the tournament, and potfuls of money — so much after taxes that you never have to ask the price of anything unless you want to.

This chapter is about comparisons:

Who

What

Where . . .

who you compare your company with, what criteria you use to compare your company with another, and where you find the information to form the basis for a comparison.

RATIOS — US VS. THEM

Bob Who?

Robert Morris helped finance the colonists through the Revolutionary War, but that's not why he's remembered. Robert Morris Associates is The National Association of

95

Bank Loan and Credit Officers, representing about 75% of U. S. commercial banking resources. Imagine all those banks and the diverse borrowers like you who arrive daily with financial statements to support their loan applications. Robert Morris collects most of these statements every year, feeds them to a computer, and out comes their series *Annual Statement Studies*, with one page of financial ratios each for hundreds of different industries (321 as of 1981). This financial profile is used by all sorts of people including your banker. Page 97 is the *Annual Statement Studies* for the AM radio station business, S.I.C. # 4832*.

What Does It All Mean, Coach?

A typical page in Robert Morris is divided into two parts. Part one is found *above* the row labeled **RATIOS**; its information is expressed as percentages summarizing assets, liabilities, owners' equity, and items from the income statement. Part two lies *below* the row labeled **RATIOS** and contains sixteen standard financial ratios.

To the left and right of the center column, which names all the classifications, are a number of vertical columns. The column farthest left headed 0-250M reports

16

information for AM radio stations whose total assets are less than $250,000. The number 16 indicates that sixteen such stations reported data. On our sample page, there are two columns reporting other size classifications ($250,000–1,000,000) and ($1,000,000–10,000,000),

All

and a fourth column headed 59, which is the financial composite of all fifty-nine stations reporting, regardless of size. By looking just above the column headings, we can determine that twenty of the fifty-nine stations reported for the period June 30–September 30, 1979 and that the other thirty-nine stations reported for the period October 1, 1979–March 31, 1980.

To the right, four additional columns represent

*S.I.C. stands for the U. S. Department of Commerce's Standard Industrial Classification numbering system.

	Current Data					Comparative Historical Data			
	20(8/30-9/30/79)		39(10/1/79-3/31/80)			6/30/75-3/31/77	6/30/77-3/31/78	6/30/78-3/31/79	6/30/79-3/31/80
ASSET SIZE	0-250M	250M-1MM	1-10MM	10-50MM	ALL	ALL	ALL	ALL	ALL
NUMBER OF STATEMENTS	16	27	13	3	59	89	81	70	59
ASSETS	%	%	%	%	%	%	%	%	%
Cash & Equivalents	5.4	7.2	5.8		6.5	8.6	6.3	9.0	6.5
Accts. & Notes Rec. - Trade(net)	23.5	19.7	16.9		19.8	19.9	19.4	20.7	19.8
Inventory	1.1	.1	.0		.4	1.1	.2	.6	.4
All Other Current	2.1	3.2	7.4		3.8	1.2	1.5	2.3	3.8
Total Current	32.2	30.2	30.1		30.5	30.8	27.4	32.5	30.5
Fixed Assets (net)	52.2	44.9	46.1		46.9	39.4	43.1	43.6	46.9
Intangibles (net)	6.9	7.4	20.4		11.2	15.2	17.1	11.4	11.2
All Other Non-Current	8.7	17.4	3.5		11.4	14.6	12.4	12.6	11.4
Total	100.0	100.0	100.0		100.0	100.0	100.0	100.0	100.0
LIABILITIES									
Notes Payable-Short Term	5.7	10.6	5.7		7.7	4.6	5.5	6.0	7.7
Cur. Mat.-L/T/D	13.8	7.4	4.0		8.3	5.7	6.2	4.5	8.3
Accts. & Notes Payable - Trade	5.2	7.5	3.6		6.0	5.2	5.8	4.7	6.0
Accrued Expenses	3.4	3.7	4.5		3.8	4.7	5.9	4.5	3.8
All Other Current	5.9	3.3	5.9		4.8	4.7	3.6	2.2	4.8
Total Current	34.0	32.5	23.8		30.3	25.0	27.0	21.9	30.3
Long Term Debt	35.9	42.7	33.7		38.5	32.8	35.9	35.6	38.5
All Other Non-Current	1.3	1.0	3.1		1.7	3.1	7.0	4.1	1.7
Net Worth	28.8	23.8	39.4		29.6	39.1	30.2	38.4	29.6
Total Liabilities & Net Worth	100.0	100.0	100.0		100.0	100.0	100.0	100.0	100.0
INCOME DATA									
Net Sales	100.0	100.0	100.0		100.0	100.0	100.0	100.0	100.0
Cost Of Sales									
Gross Profit									
Operating Expenses	98.5	89.0	86.4		90.3	88.6	95.5	84.3	90.3
Operating Profit	1.5	11.0	13.6		9.7	11.4	4.5	15.7	9.7
All Other Expenses (net)	-.3	4.7	6.2		3.6	4.6	4.0	5.9	3.6
Profit Before Taxes	1.8	6.3	7.4		6.1	6.8	.6	9.8	6.1
RATIOS									
Current	2.2	1.8	2.1		1.9	2.0	1.8	2.4	1.9
	1.2	1.0	1.6		1.2	1.2	1.1	1.6	1.2
	.6	.5	.6		.6	.8	.7	1.2	.6
Quick	1.9	1.6	1.9		1.8	2.0	1.6	2.3	1.8
	1.1	.9	1.2		1.1	1.1	1.0	1.5	1.1
	.6	.5	.4		.5	.8	.7	1.0	.5
Sales/Receivables	40 9.2	44 8.3	41 8.8	42 8.7		49 7.5	50 7.3	45 8.1	42 8.7
	53 6.9	61 6.0	58 6.3	56 6.5		57 6.4	59 6.2	54 6.7	56 6.5
	64 5.7	66 5.5	66 5.5	66 5.5		73 5.0	69 5.3	64 5.7	66 5.5
Cost of Sales/Inventory									
Sales/Working Capital	10.2	9.1	7.3		8.0	6.4	8.8	6.9	8.0
	21.2	INF	12.7		21.9	23.7	96.7	11.0	21.9
	-9.0	-5.2	-9.3		-9.4	-30.5	-13.2	34.6	-9.4
EBIT/Interest	5.7	3.4	6.1		5.8	7.2	5.0	10.0	5.8
	(15) 2.0	(22) 1.5	(12) 4.4	(52) 2.2		(65) 3.1	(64) 2.2	(53) 3.5	(52) 2.2
	1.1	.3	-.1		.7	1.5	.3	2.1	.7
Cash Flow/Cur. Mat. L/T/D	2.1	2.9			3.1	5.7	2.8	6.1	3.1
	(11) .9	(10) 1.9		(32) 1.6		(45) 2.3	(47) 1.4	(39) 3.0	(32) 1.6
	.6	.8			.6	.9	.3	1.7	.6
Fixed/Worth	.9	.8	.8		.9	.6	.9	.8	.9
	1.5	2.7	2.6		2.6	1.5	2.2	1.6	2.6
	-35.8	-5.9	-6.8		-10.0	-36.0	-6.0	8.0	-10.0
Debt/Worth	.9	.7	1.1		.9	.6	1.2	.7	.9
	2.0	4.6	3.5		4.1	2.2	3.1	2.3	4.1
	-99.5	-11.6	-12.0		-15.4	-46.4	-11.8	11.0	-15.4
% Profit Before Taxes/Tangible Net Worth	58.3	50.0		(41) 57.0		67.1	81.8	88.2	57.0
	(11) 10.4	(19) 18.7		25.0		(65) 35.5	(55) 23.7	(55) 47.1	(41) 25.0
	-4.2	-20.0		-3.1		16.2	4.4	24.1	-3.1
% Profit Before Taxes/Total Assets	11.5	13.3	22.3		16.3	22.6	16.0	21.1	16.3
	3.4	4.8	16.3		7.2	9.2	6.7	10.9	7.2
	-1.4	-2.6	-4.6		-1.9	2.0	-2.7	5.5	-1.9
Sales/Net Fixed Assets	7.3	4.4	5.2		4.4	5.2	4.4	4.6	4.4
	2.7	2.4	1.9		2.6	3.2	2.8	3.4	2.6
	2.1	1.8	1.5		1.8	1.8	1.7	1.8	1.8
Sales/Total Assets	2.0	1.6	1.2		1.6	1.6	1.4	1.7	1.6
	1.6	1.1	1.1		1.1	1.1	1.1	1.2	1.1
	1.1	.8	1.0		1.0	.8	.8	.9	1.0
% Depr., Dep., Amort./Sales	2.1	3.4	3.7		3.5	2.9	3.3	2.9	3.5
	4.3	5.4	(11) 6.3	(57) 5.4		(82) 5.3	(69) 4.9	(57) 4.9	5.4
	8.2	6.9	9.4		8.1	8.2	7.7	8.3	8.1
% Lease & Rental Exp/Sales	.9				.8	1.1	1.0	.8	.8
	(13) 1.9		(25) 1.9			(32) 1.6	(37) 1.8	(33) 1.5	(25) 1.9
	4.5				4.5	2.9	3.3	3.1	4.5
% Officers' Comp/Sales	5.0				6.5	4.6	5.7	7.8	6.5
	(11) 7.2		(19) 10.2			(32) 7.2	(31) 8.2	(20) 10.0	(19) 10.2
	16.0				19.3	11.9	10.6	16.4	19.3
Net Sales ($)	3723M	16473M	33877M	42328M	96401M	166317M	170380M	116864M	96401M
Total Assets ($)	2363M	13437M	31866M	42783M	90269M	193043M	163606M	100829M	90269M

M = $thousand   MM = $million
See Pages 1 through 10 for Explanation of Ratios and Data

Services - AM Radio Stations, SIC #4832†

historical data from prior years. The right-hand set of four columns lets us see trends developing over the recent past in the industry.

†On page 239 you will find some very useful information from the Robert Morris Associates governing the use of this information.

Everything's Up to Date in Kansas
City — Including the Current
Ratios

Now look on the left side at the small boldface square. It contains information on one of the most commonly used financial ratios, the *current* ratio. Just as in Chapter 2, this is nothing more than a firm's current assets divided by its current liabilities as a measure of ability to pay its current debts. In the square, we see three pieces of data describing current ratios of firms with $250,000 to $1,000,000 in total assets; what these three pieces of information mean can be explained with a simple diagram:

	Highest value in the distribution	This information is not reported by Robert Morris *Annual Statement Studies.*
	Upper quartile (point at which the top 25% of the distribution begins)	In the boldface square, the value 1.8 represents that current ratio above which only 25% of the reporting companies have a higher one.
The distribution of the current ratios of all 27 firms in this size category	Median (point separating the two halves of the distribution)	In the distribution, the value 1.0 represents the current ratio in the middle of the 27 reporting companies.
	Lower quartile (point at which the lower 25% of the distribution begins)	In the boldface square, the value .5 represents that current ratio below which only 25% of the reporting companies have a lower one.
	Lowest value in the distribution	This information is not reported by Robert Morris *Annual Statement Studies.*

Do You See the Beauty of It?

With three pieces of information about current ratios of twenty-nine AM radio stations having $250,000 to $1,000,000 of total assets, you can tell a great deal more about current ratios in this industry than you could if you had only one current ratio summarizing all fifty-nine AM stations regardless of their size.

Days and Ratios — Now I'm
Really Confused

Now look back at our Robert Morris page again to the small boldface circle. We are in a new category, sales divided by accounts receivable. The three boldface numbers in the circle, 58, are days, derived from the three values just to
    41
circle, 58, are days, derived from the three values just to
    66
the right of the ones in the circle. Sales divided by receivables is a basic measure of how good you are at collecting your accounts receivable; for example, the 6.3 value tells us that the median company (the one in the middle) has annual sales equal to 6.3 times its receivables. Turned upside down, it has 1/6.3 or 15.9% of its annual sales in receivables. The boldface value 58 in the circle simply converts this 15.9% into days, like this: 15.9% × 365 days = 58 days. Voila! On average, this company collects the money from its sales about 58 days after billing. So we can have this ratio in the form of a number (6.3), a percentage (15.9), or in days (58). Very useful.

    Now look at the figure (19) in the boldface diamond at the bottom of our sample Robert Morris page. This value tells the number of companies that reported information whenever the number is less than the number heading the entire column. We know from the column heading that fifty-nine companies provided information for this column; however, the value (19) shows that only nineteen of those fifty-nine companies provided any information on the ratio of their officers' compensation to their total sales. Whenever you see a value in parentheses like this, it means that fewer than the total number of reporting companies have provided a particular piece of information.

Forewarned Is Forearmed

The Robert Morris Associates' *Annual Statement Studies* gives bank loan officers quick access to the financial profile of a wide variety of industries — probably including yours. So when you walk through that banker's door to ask for a loan, he or she can compare *your* financial statement with others, and come to some conclusion as to how you're doing. But, here's the good news; you can get the very same information by trotting down to your local business school library and pulling *Annual Statement Studies* off the shelf. Or you can order a copy of your own by writing to Robert Morris Associates, 1616 Philadelphia National Bank Building, Philadelphia, Pa. 19107. Sort of evens things up.

Robert Morris, Meet Leo Troy

If you don't like trotting out of your office to get this information, or if your company is located in Iron City, Nevada, 256 miles from the nearest business school library, you can purchase a book with similar information — specifically, *Almanac of Business and Industrial Financial Ratios*, by Leo Troy, available from Prentice-Hall, Inc., Englewood Cliffs, N. J. (who, by the way, are also the fearless entrepreneurs who published the raffish little book you are now reading).

Dr. Troy updates his book every year, so you can buy the latest information rather easily. Dr. Troy's source of information is the tax returns of companies filed with the IRS; his book is a compendium of financial information on approximately 170 different categories of companies. One very interesting and useful feature of Dr. Troy's book is the two different performance categories for

reporting. First he reports information on all companies in a particular industrial grouping whether they made a profit or not. Then, on a separate page, he reports only those companies in that industrial grouping that did make a profit.

Look on the next page for a sample from Dr. Troy's book; you'll see a whole lot of financial information on profitable companies in the lumber and construction materials business. From the row headed "Number of establishments" you can determine by looking under column A — just like a Chinese restaurant — that 6,947 companies provided the information from which this page was distilled. Wow! That's a lot more companies than the 59 AM radio stations we were dealing with in *Robert Morris*. And looking across the top row from columns B through I, we see that Dr. Troy has provided us with eight size categories among those 6,947 companies. Applying the Lord giveth and taketh away doctrine, however, we find the information in the body of the table to be not quite as detailed as that we got from *Robert Morris;* for instance, no statistical distribution in the form of medians and upper and lower quartiles. (Most of you will probably shout with joy at that loss.) Furthermore, Dr. Troy provides fewer ratios than does Robert Morris Associates. For example, you won't find information on asset turnovers (i.e., total sales divided by total assets).

What's in It for You

Well, if you run a company in a fairly standard line of business and want to compare yourself with others in that business, both Robert Morris Associates and Dr. Troy will help you considerably. On the other hand, if you manufacture corrugated steel pipe, maple flooring, or fabricated roof trusses, or if you install ceiling tiles, neither Robert Morris nor Dr. Troy has anything you can draw a bead on.

But wait. You still may not be alone with your ratios. Isn't there a national association for *everything* in the United States — folks who collect hummingbird eggs, folks who save only large stamps colored blue, and perhaps

Corporations with Net Income:
Wholesale Trade, Miscellaneous Wholesale Trade,
Lumber and Construction Materials

	A	B	C	D	E	F	G	H	I
					Size of Assets in Thousands of Dollars (000 omitted)				
Item Description for Accounting Period 7/74 Through 6/75	Total	Under $100	$100 to 250	$250 to 500	$500 to 1,000	$1,000 to 5,000	$5,000 to 10,000	$10,000 to 25,000	$25,000 to 50,000
1. Number of establishments	6,947	1,752	1,566	1,438	1,213	891	56	21	10
2. Total receipts ($ millions)	14,175.6	352.9	857.7	1,867.5	2,923.0	4,941.6	1,260.1	683.0	1,289.8
			Selected Operating Factors as Percentage of Net Sales						
3. Cost of operations	81.2	73.4	79.2	77.3	79.7	81.3	84.8	82.4	89.6
4. Compensation of officers	2.2	6.4	3.7	3.3	2.5	1.9	1.0	.8	.4
5. Repairs	.3	.1	.4	.3	.3	.3	.3	.2	.1
6. Bad debts	.4	.3	.3	.5	.6	.4	.2	.4	.2
7. Rent on business property	.5	.8	.8	.5	.6	.5	.3	.5	.3
8. Taxes (excl. federal tax)	1.1	1.4	1.3	1.3	1.3	1.1	.9	1.1	.6
9. Interest	1.0	.5	.6	.4	.7	.8	.6	1.3	3.8
10. Deprec., deplet., amortiz.†	.8	.9	.8	1.0	.8	.8	.8	.9	.8
11. Advertising	.2	.3	.2	.2	.3	.2	.1	.2	.3
12. Pensions and other benefit plans	.5	1.0	.2	.4	.5	.5	.4	.5	.2
13. Other expenses	9.8	11.8	10.4	11.2	10.6	9.9	8.8	7.8	6.0
14. Net profit before tax	2.1	3.0	2.2	3.5	2.1	2.4	1.8	3.9	#

†Depreciation largest factor.

Adapted from Leo Troy, *Almanac of Business and Industrial Financial Ratios*, 1978 edition (Englewood Cliffs, N.J.: Prentice-Hall, Inc., 1978), Table II, p. 211.

Corporations with Net Income:
Wholesale Trade, Miscellaneous Wholesale Trade,
Lumber and Construction Materials (Continued)

Item Description for Accounting Period 7/74 Through 6/75	A Total	B Under $100	C $100 to 250	D $250 to 500	E $500 to 1,000	F $1,000 to 5,000	G $5,000 to 10,000	H $10,000 to 25,000	I $25,000 to 50,000
Size of Assets in Thousands of Dollars (000 omitted)									
Selected Financial Ratios (number of times ratio is to one)									
15. Current ratio	1.9	2.1	2.1	2.3	2.0	1.9	1.9	2.1	1.3
16. Quick ratio	1.1	1.5	1.4	1.5	1.1	1.1	1.1	1.1	.8
17. Net sales to net working capital	8.5	11.7	7.7	8.2	8.5	8.5	10.0	6.8	8.3
18. Net sales to net worth	6.5	12.4	5.6	6.4	7.4	6.5	5.8	4.6	7.0
19. Inventory turnover	8.4	25.2	8.4	10.4	8.9	7.8	7.9	6.9	12.0
20. Total liabilities to net worth	1.2	1.3	.8	.8	1.2	1.1	.8	1.0	3.3
Selected Financial Factors in Percentages									
21. Current liabilities to net worth	89.2	93.6	64.7	59.2	86.7	81.5	64.4	63.6	—
22. Inventory to current assets	36.6	26.0	33.0	35.1	41.2	40.6	38.7	41.1	24.1
23. Net income to net worth	17.0	40.6	17.9	23.7	16.3	16.3	11.2	19.5	11.8
24. Retained earnings to net income	45.9	54.1	87.2	39.1	86.3	82.8	85.4	—	81.7

even folks who manufacture corrugated steel pipe? Right you are, and you get an "A" for brilliance. There *is* such an association for corrugated steel pipe manufacturers. It's called the NCSPA, the National Corrugated Steel Pipe Association; it's headquartered near Chicago, Illinois; and it's headed up by a very bright young man, let's say John.

John happens to believe that associations ought to have a good bash when they go off to resorts for their annual convention, but he also knows that, if having fun is all your association does in Atlantic City or Lake Tahoe or wherever, it won't be much help to the members, and it surely won't last long. So John busies himself collecting financial information every year from his member manufacturers of corrugated steel pipe, then works with a national accounting firm to sort, tabulate, and array that information in useful form, which he distributes to his association members. John's not alone. I personally work with seventeen associations to design and offer seminars in accounting, finance, and tax, all seventeen of which do the same thing as John at NCSPA. And I imagine there are at least a thousand others who do it too.

The ability to compare yourself with others is one of the real benefits of belonging to an association. (If your association director doesn't like this and doesn't provide the information, fire him. That's right, fire him.) In this particular instance, the NCSPA publishes an annual ratio survey with two different size categories. You'd love it — it includes all the terrific statistical information *Robert Morris* gives you too — oh, joy! This survey then becomes the basis of the NCSPA annual financial management seminar as well as provides members with a yardstick for comparing their operating results with those of all the other folks in the corrugated steel pipe business. Sort of like checking around the locker room, an adult version.

Caveat Lector

Ratio analysis is an excellent tool, but there are problems with using ratios that do not meet the eye. In the first place, folks tend to report information from their historic financial records and not from their market value balance sheets. Furthermore, many surveys don't tell enough about the officers' compensation package for us to know what is profit and what is before-tax salary taken out. And few people ever report information that didn't come from their books kept for taxes — but we're not the IRS.

In short, there are an awful lot of ways people keep books, and ratio surveys sort of have to put all those together into one pot to calculate ratios. And I haven't even mentioned the problem of geographic cost differentials — you know, it costs more in labor to manufacture wooden pallets in Midlands, Michigan, than it does in Midnight, Mississippi, so comparisons of Midnight and Midlands are often odious. Neither do we know from most studies about who owns the real estate, how much money the kids are paid in salaries for work they don't do, or who keeps up the house at the beach, the airplane, and the five cars. Finally, many ratio studies are static. That is, they don't show trends over long enough periods of time to reveal consequential events and forces that may be acting on an industry. To say it another way, looking at last year may win the battle for you but lose the war if you are in the buggy whip business. Get it? *Conclusion:* Ratios aren't perfect, but they're better than stark ignorance.

Once More with Feeling

If there weren't a size 36-D, a 32-AA might be considered downright bosomy! If there weren't a par, I and a million other folks would be a hell of a golfer. Yeah, and if there weren't a company in your line of business that made 45% after taxes on investment, your 9% might look heroic. Alas, we all pale next to the champion — ratios give us two things: (1) a way of determining how we are measuring up to other folks who do the same kinds of things we do for a living and (2) a method of examining our financial performance in an orderly way, moving through our operation step by step. If we have *not* measured up, chances are that we can find the reasons somewhere in our books. That, gentle reader, is the subject of the second part of this chapter: how to conduct such a step-by-step analysis of your company.

TRACKING THE GREAT ELUSIVE
PROFIT MONSTER

Our procedure will be to go back to Chapter 2 and reproduce Bay Area Corrugated's balance sheet and income statement for its latest reported year. Then we will reproduce for you part of the ratio analysis provided to Bay Area, Inc., by its national association, the National Corrugated Steel Pipe Association (NCSPA to its friends). Then we'll go through a step-by-step analysis of Bay's balance sheet and income statement using industry ratios as the basis for comparison. Finally, we'll suggest some things Bay could do to improve its performance. During all this, we'll make some off-color comments about people we know, the meanings of these ratios, mistakes folks make in their interpretation and use, and what it all means for national defense. Up, up, and away!

The NCSPA reports the median (middle) value for each ratio and also the *highest* and *lowest* value for all those firms that participated in the ratio study this year. This gives us something that good old *Robert Morris* doesn't (i.e., who was best and who was worst as opposed to the *Robert Morris* report of upper and lower quartiles).

TRACKING THE GREAT ELUSIVE
PROFIT MONSTER . . . OFF WE GO

How'd We Do, Coach? Ratios 10 and 14

Net Profit to Net Sales: First thing we do, we find out how we did — and how we did starts with ratio 10, net profit before taxes divided by net sales. In Bay's case this turns out to be $620,000 \div $24,000,000 = 2.6\%$. Ow. A quick look back at the ranges reported for ratio 10 on the preced-

Balance Sheet
Bay Area Corrugated Pipe, Inc.
December 31, 19X2

Assets

Current assets			
Cash	$ 560,000		
Marketable securities	80,000		
Accounts receivable			
(net of est. bad debts)	4,600,000		
Inventory	7,200,000		
Prepaid expenses	160,000		
Total Current Assets			$12,600,000
Fixed assets			
Land			200,000
Fabrication shop and office	2,500,000		
Furniture	50,000		
Trucks and machinery	1,700,000		
Less: Accumulated		4,250,000	
depreciation		1,050,000	
Net fixed assets			3,200,000
Total fixed assets			$3,400,000
Total assets			$16,000,000

Liabilities

Current liabilities		
Accounts payable	4,420,000	
Notes payable	1,930,000	
Accrued expense	280,000	
Long-term note		
(current portion)	700,000	
Total current liabilities		$7,330,000
Long-term liabilities		
Mortgage note payable		2,800,000
Total liabilities		$10,130,000

Equity

Capital stock		500,000
Retained earnings		5,370,000
Total equity		$5,870,000

109

Trail Sign Profit and Loss

Income Statement
Bay Area Corrugated Pipe, Inc.
Year Ended December 31, 19X2

Gross Sales	$24,800,000	
Less: Returns and allowances	800,000	
Net sales		$24,000,000
Expenses		
Cost of goods sold	19,100,000	
Depreciation	680,000	
Sales and administrative expense	2,690,000	
		22,470,000
Operating profit		$ 1,530,000
Less: Interest		910,000
Net profit before taxes		$ 620,000
Provisions for income taxes		300,000
Net profit after taxes		$ 320,000

Signs of Other Hunters

NCSPA Ratio Analysis, 19X2
(abbreviated, firms with over $5,000,000 sales)

	Highest	Median	Lowest
1. Quick ratio	4.3	1.1	.4
2. Current ratio	9.4	1.8	1.0
3. Receivables turnover	11.8	9.9	5.2
4. Inventory turnover	15.9	6.3	2.7
5. Asset turnover	5.2	2.7	1.5
6. Noninterest-bearing current liabilities to total assets (%)	29.7	13.4	2.6
7. Lo. 1-term debt to stockholders' equity	3.9	.4	0
8. Fixed asset turnover	19.1	13.7	7.5
9. Current asset turnover	4.4	3.3	1.9
10. Net profit before tax to net sales (%)	10.8	6.7	2.2
11. Cost of goods (%)	81.5	77.8	74.3
12. Selling and administrative expense (%)	19.2	13.7	5.3
13. Financing costs (%)	4.0	1.7	.8
14. Net profit before tax to stockholders' equity (%)	52.4	24.9	8.5
15. Net profit before tax to total assets (%)	23.9	15.3	3.9
16. Working capital turnover	16.1	6.9	2.3

ing page indicates that we are definitely below the median but not the worst reporting company. A near miss. Our profit to sales performance is less than half of the median (which is 6.7%) and about a quarter of the best performer (10.8%). Definitely lots of room for improvement.

Note, however, that we need to be sure that we have measured company profit here and not excessive diddling. If we employ nine relatives, pay ourselves $50,000 a year more than the job is actually worth, and diddle for another $50,000 a year (cars, boat, plane, travel, etc.), then let's be careful — our corporation's profit is probably greatly understated. The president of Bay, Inc., reminds himself that his salary is $25,000 lower than what he heard at the convention this spring and that he hasn't done much diddling at all in the last three years. Thus it's safe to conclude that 2.6% is *not* a sterling performance, and something is amiss.

Net Profit Before Taxes to Stockholders' Equity: Let's double-check our profit to sales performance by looking at what our *equity* in the corporation actually earns. Of course, we want to earn profit dollars, but profit alone is not the name of the game in business today. What we have to do is earn enough on our *equity* in the company — otherwise we might as well take it out, invest it in tax-free bonds, buy a 42-foot Bertram, and head for the Gulf Stream. Look now at ratio 14, before-tax return on stockholders' equity. The industry median is 24.9%, with a high and low of 52.4% and 8.5%, respectively. Ours at Bay is $620,000 ÷ $5,870,000 = 10.6%, pretty far down toward the low end of the distribution. Not good news at all, especially at times when tax-free municipals earn about the same. Better call our business broker and put in an order for the Bertram. Hold it! Give us a couple more pages before we do anything rash.

Are They Working out There?
Ratio 11

Cost of Goods: Unless Bay, Inc., is guilty of underpricing, the rather miserable profit performance ought to be explained out in the plant (production costs), in the office (out of control selling and administrative expenses), or in financing (interest costs). First, go out to the plant for a look.

Ratio 11 for NCSPA shows a median cost of goods of 77.8%, with a high of 81.5% and a low of 74.3%. Bay, Inc., comes in at $19,100,000 ÷ $24,000,000 = 79.6%, so we're in the ballpark here. Maybe there's some room for improvement, but clearly cost of goods is not the reason for our lousy profit to sales performance. We make a mental note to spend Saturday morning with the plant foreman and work up some cost reduction goals for the spring. Then we go back to our witch-hunt.

*Who's in Charge of Peddling
and Bookkeeping? Ratio 12*

Selling and Administrative Expense: We duck inside the office for a comparative look, armed with industry information on ratio 12, selling and administrative costs. We remind ourselves that the industry practice is to *include* depreciation here, so we'll have to do the same to get comparability. We see that the industry median here is 13.7%, with a high and low of 19.2% and 5.3%, respectively. Our own selling and administrative expense (including depreciation) is $2,690,000 + $680,000 ÷ $24,000,000 = 14.0%, so we seem to be right in the middle of the pack. Could we improve anyhow? Maybe those selling expenses do need controlling after all, and I wonder if we've got to have *all* those folks working in the office. Never considered that each extra administrative employee adds almost .1% to this ratio. Damn! And we've got 19, no — added cousin Joey last week — make that 20 working in the office right now.

Bankers Dues Maybe: Ratio 13

Financing Costs: With increasing interest rates, many associations have begun the practice of breaking out financing costs. This is an excellent practice for two reasons: (1) it raises the visibility of financing costs, and (2) it moves your attention from the income statement to the balance sheet. The balance sheet is where you *must* look if you are ever going to find the reason for high financing costs. OK, pipemakers, let's look at interest expense as a percentage of net sales in our industry. The middle of the distribution is at 1.7%, with a high and a low of 4.0% and .8%, respectively. We can cipher our financing cost quickly as $910,000 interest expense ÷ sales of $24,000,000 = 3.8%, which puts us right up there with the Big Borrower. Red flag for sure — looks as if there's too much money borrowed. And, dammit, we have those enormous retained earnings inside the business sup-posedly doing their part to finance it too. Something ain't right.

Time out

Seventh inning stretch, time to look back, to get the score up to date and see how far we've come. OK, here's what we've found so far:

1. Our profit to sales ratio of 2.6% needs to come up to 6.7% *just* to get us to the middle of the pack in our industry. That means 6.7% − 2.6% = 4.1% lower cost as a goal.

2. Our cost of goods at 79.6% is almost two percentage points higher than the industry median of 77.8%, or 79.6% − 77.8% = 1.8%. Suppose we get this item down to the me-dian. Then 4.1% lower cost − 1.8% reduced cost of goods = 2.3% cost reduction left to go. Gettin' there slowly.

3. Our sales and administration expense ratio of 14.0% is .3% above the median. Not much change; 2.3% to go − .3% potential reduction here still leaves 2.0% yet to be cut.

4. Our financing costs are 3.8% of sales, and the industry median is only 1.7%. The potential cut here just to get down to the middle of the pack is 3.8% − 1.7% = 2.1%. So if we could do it, our 2.0% to go − 2.1% potential cut here brings us about even with the board.

Some Conclusions at This Point

Not to run around, get drunk, sing with joy, and buy a hand-held calculator to cipher more ratios, no sir!! What we've said and done is full of assumptions, watch:

1. We've assumed Bay, Inc., wants to operate at least as well as the median industry company.

2. We've assumed Bay, Inc., management wants (read that "has the guts and drive") to do whatever it takes to get there.

3. We've assumed Bay's financial statements and ratios *are* comparable with the industry ratios.

4. We have not assumed that Bay wants to accomplish anything *more* than a *median* performance, which may be the most cynical assumption we've made.

5. We've taken a mechanical, that is, numerical, perspective on the whole comparison so far. We've assumed that, if others do it, then Bay can do it. Well, this may be safe when the goal is only to be as good as the median. Take heart — the median golf score for those who play regularly is 101.

6. What can we assume about personnel? We've said nothing about Bay's people. If the company is full of room-temperature I.Q. twits, not even an enlightened management can raise company performance much — probably not even to the median. Leading a bunch of twits with one person doing all the work isn't much of anything!

7. And watch this one. Reducing cost of goods a point or two and getting rid of a couple of drone salespersons and firing one or two twits out of your office is child's play. But re-arranging your balance sheet so that you don't need to borrow all that damn money or use all those retained earnings is big league — hard to do. So, hang on. Even if Bay, Inc., gets on its horse, races through the forests of production and selling and administration, killing all the dragons as it goes, all it will have is three quarters of the solution to its desired return of 6.7% on sales. Getting the other one quarter to complete the solution will require management to go to work on the balance sheet. After all, if you owe all that money and use all those retained earnings, it must be because you have a lot of assets to use it on. Simple as that. So hang on to your hat while we race around the balance sheet and look for damsels in distress there. (And you thought we had it all wrapped up.)

TRACKING THE GREAT
ELUSIVE PROFIT MONSTER
DOWN A NEW PATH

Feast or Famine: Ratios 5 and 15

Asset Turnovers: The asset turnover ratio has come in for increased scrutiny lately for a good reason: it costs too much money to finance a lot of current and fixed assets.

Just look how Bay, Inc., is suffering. As a result, folks at financial society luncheons have begun to talk "asset management." In plain English, they mean keeping just enough of everything on hand to do business and nothing more. No surpluses of anything. Running lean.

To get asset turnover, you divide total sales by total assets. In Bay's case this is $24,000,000 ÷ $16,000,000 = 1.5. Now what've we got? The value 1.5 can be thought of as indicating that Bay gets $1.50 of sales out of every $1.00 it has invested in assets. (If this point isn't transparently clear, just take it as an article of faith now, and wait one more chapter. Chapter 6 goes into so much excruciating detail on this very point that, by the time you've finished reading it, you will know more about asset turns than you *ever* wanted to learn. So for now, take it as given.)

Let's look at the industry study. Ooops! Bay is all the way at the bottom, the lowest in the whole corrugated pipe industry in asset turns: 1.5 turns for Bay versus the industry median of 2.7. This tells us the median company gets $2.70 of sales out of every dollar of its assets and that the top company gets $5.20 (an asset turn of 5.2). Now there's a screaming indictment. Bay, Inc., is the absolute pits when it comes to asset management, with *too damn many assets* ($16,000,000 net book value) for its sales volume ($24,000,000). No wonder it has to borrow all that money and keep all those retained earnings in the company. Look at what it uses to make pipe — $16,000,000 worth of plant and equipment and inventory. Somebody has to pay for them!

Net Profit Before Taxes on Total Assets: Another cut at the issue of asset management can be taken by using ratio 15. In Bay's case, net profit before taxes on total assets turns out to be $620,000 ÷ $16,000,000 = 3.9%, meaning that every dollar of assets Bay has invested earns a return of less than 4% before tax. The industry median here is 15.3%, with a high of 23.9% and a low of — that's right, you guessed it — Bay's own 3.9%. "Lord, help them," you say, "they don't earn enough on their assets to pay for financing them — they'd do better putting the whole mess in something that earned more than 4% before taxes and go fishing." Right on, I say, you're learning fast! But whoa just a second. If your salary of $145,617.87 came out before taxes and if you're paying for a beach and a mountain house through the company, and if you just bought a Lear 55 — "Wait, wait," you say, "I read Chapter 2. I think I'll stay in the pipe business and try to clean it up some more . . . then maybe sell it."

Where Have All the Assets Gone?
Ratios 8 and 9

Fixed Asset Turnover: Everything's gotta be somewhere, assets too! If they ain't here, they gotta be there; it's as simple as that. Oh yeah, I forgot the automobile dealer's fence (the one the IRS field auditor found around the dealer's house instead of around his sales lot). OK, fixed assets: if they ain't here and they ain't there, then maybe they're out at the lake. But, hell, even out there someone has to get the money to pay for them. Ratio 8, fixed asset turnover, is just a refinement of ratio 5, which gave us total asset turnover. Ratio 8 for Bay, Inc., is total sales divided by net *fixed* assets, or $24,000,000 ÷ $3,200,000 = 7.5. This translates into how many sales Bay manages to get out of every dollar of its fixed assets. Checking out the industry study, we quickly see that Bay's fixed asset turnover of 7.5 is a winner again, but in the wrong race. With an industry median fixed asset turnover of 13.7 and a top performance of 19.1 turns, Bay comes a cropper here. The obvious conclusion: far too much invested in plant and machinery.

So what would it take Bay to get back in the race and draw even with the median firm at its fixed asset turnover of 13.7? One alternative would be for Bay to operate at its current sales level of $24,000,000 with

$$\frac{\$24,000,000}{13.7} = \$1,751,825 \text{ of fixed assets}$$

or roughly half of what it has now. Looking at it from the other perspective Bay could do

$ 3,200,000   (Bay's fixed assets at present)
× 13.7
$43,840,000   (Worth of business)

on its present fixed asset base. So you say the first alternative will be the easier one to implement, that is, doing about the same sales volume on fewer assets. Well, you may be right; Bay could always start by selling the plant to the family and leasing it back (we'll cover the smart way to do this in Chapter 8). Regardless of which direction Bay heads off in, it's clear that it has too many fixed assets for the volume it does. Maybe Bay needs to call the truck dealer and cancel its order for that new eighteen-wheeler.

Current Asset Turnover: Look now at ratio 9. For Bay, Inc., we calculate this turnover to be $24,000,000 ÷ $12,600,000 current assets = 1.9 turns. By now you know what this means: Bay does about $1.90 in sales off every dollar it has in current assets. What does the industry do? Well, we see a median current asset turnover of 3.3, with a high of 4.4, and poor old Bay at the bottom of the heap reporting a 1.9. It's obvious this time that Bay has too much tied up in current assets for its volume. Exactly where those excess current assets are is the subject of the next section.

When Is Enough Too Much?
Ratios 1 and 2

The quick ratio, 1, and the current ratio, 2, measure the adequacy of current assets. The current ratio tells us whether we have enough current assets on hand (i.e., cash, marketable securities, notes receivable, accounts receivable, inventory, and prepaid expense) to pay our current liabilities. It is calculated in Bay's case by taking

Cash	$ 560,000
Marketable securities	80,000
Accounts receivable	4,600,000
Inventory	7,200,000
Prepaid expense	160,000
	$12,600,000

and comparing this $12,600,000 with Bay's current liabilities of $7,330,000, this way:

$$\text{Current ratio} = \frac{\$12,600,000}{\$\ 7,330,000} = 1.7$$

You can read that 1.7 as $1.70 of current assets for every $1.00 of current liabilities. A quick look at the industry ratios brings joy. At last, here's a ratio we need not be ashamed of. With an industry median of 1.8, a high of 9.4 and a low of 1.0, Bay, Inc., is somewhere in the bottom half, but not at the very bottom. What a relief!

Is 1.7 enough? That's the question. The answer is a firm *yes!* At least it's yes everywhere you look except in accounting books and bankers' minds. Bankers love a high current ratio because it assures them of being paid back their short-term loans. Bankers begin to get smiles when the current ratio goes above 2.0. And many good accounting books suggest that a current ratio of at least 2.0 is a worthy goal. Bull! It's a good goal only if you're working for the bank or for your accountant, but *not* otherwise.

Getting your current ratio up to and above 2.0 takes too many current assets, and you know now what *that* does for return on stockholders' equity. Getting a current ratio to 2.0 relieves your banker of worry and relieves your accountant from doing some of the important, nonbean-counting tasks he should be working on every day. But it does absolutely nothing for you.

For an example of the absolute absurdity of a current ratio that high for all companies, look at the case of a chain of convenience stores that sells for cash, replenishes its inventory at least once a week, and gets thirty days from its suppliers to pay for the inventory. Now just what sense does it make for it to have a current ratio much over 1.0? In fact, it makes no sense. Maybe that's why Hop-In Stores, Inc., a successful publicly held convenience store chain in Virginia reported a current ratio of *less than* 1.0 on one of its year-end statements. Nothing to worry about — if you're paying your bills on time, whatever you got is enough. Doctrinaire views on current ratios of 2.0 and above are best saved for accounting professors and bankers, neither guaranteed to know much about business anyhow!

To be sure, your banker may pressure you to get your current ratio up near 2.0, but if you can diddle, as we talked about in Chapter 2, then you can diddle your banker here too. Bay's current ratio is even a tad high, I'd say. The industry high here is 9.4, which is purely absurd! The only possible justification I can think of is that they've just collected a lot of bills and have inventoried the money for a while.

Quick, Quicker, Quickest

Folks often compute another form of the current ratio called the quick ratio. It's just like the current ratio except that you count as "quick current assets" only cash, marketable securities, short-term notes receivable, and accounts receivable. (You leave out inventory, not a quick asset to dispose of.) In Bay's case, the total of quick current assets is

Cash	$ 560,000
Marketable securities	80,000
Accounts receivable	4,600,000
	$5,240,000

When we compare this with current liabilities, we get

$$\text{Quick ratio} = \frac{\text{Quick current assets}}{\text{Current liabilities}} = \frac{\$5,180,000}{7,330,000} = .71$$

So Bay has 71 cents of quick current assets with which to pay every dollar of its current liabilities. Guess what your banker would like you to have: 1.0 of course. And authors of accounting books even say such things as, "It is generally deemed prudent to have a quick ratio of at least 1.0." Look, it comes down to whether you're working for yourself or working for your banker or working for some professor with holes in his shoes who wrote an accounting book. You figure it out. I say that Bay's quick ratio is just fine, maybe even high. Look at the industry study. It's clear Bay isn't on the bottom either.

Firms seem to get along just fine with quick ratios of much less than 1.0 in spite of accounting books. In fact, half the corrugated pipe industry has a quick ratio of less than 1.1. Figures don't lie. It all comes down to this: What current assets do you need to pay your bills on time? If a quick ratio of .6 is enough, so be it. If you need 1.0, do it! Just remember that, anytime you get a quick ratio or a current ratio higher than whatever you need, you are reducing your asset turns, enabling your banker to sleep better, relieving your internal accounting professionals from doing their job, and generally rewarding everybody but the equity holders in the crowd. Run lean. Less is more.

Partners in Crime: Ratios 3 and 4

Receivables and Inventory: The two largest entries in the current assets column for most companies are accounts receivable and inventory. And when you find a company like Bay, Inc., with its current asset turns out of control, the reason is found somewhere between receivables and inventory.

It's easy to calculate receivables turnover. All you do is divide sales by receivables: $24,000,000 \div $4,600,000 = 5.2. This figure is quickly converted into days by dividing it into 365: 365 \div 5.2 = 70.2 days' sales are in receivables. This means that, on average, Bay's accounts receivable are outstanding for almost two and a half months — and that's a bunch. The older you let your receivables get before you collect them, the more money you have to borrow to finance the company. (And since you aren't using your customers' money, you have to use your own.) *And* the longer you wait to collect them, the less collectible they become. All the studies show that; folks just forget about paying you after awhile.

The industry ratio analysis indicates a median receivables turnover of 9.9, with a low of 5.2 and a high of 11.8. You guessed right again. Bay, Inc., comes up a cropper here, winning the industry prize for worst performance of a long-running comedy. For comparison, look at the industry high of 11.8 and convert that to days: $365 \div 11.8 = 30.9$ days. Somebody collects the receivables every month, just the way they're billed! Look at Bay's situation from another perspective.

If Bay got on the ball and collected its bills so that it reached even the median receivables turnover of 9.9 — say, 10.0 to make the arithmetic simple — then Bay could get by with $\$24,000,000 \div 10.0 = \$2,400,000$ in receivables instead of its present $4,600,000. This is a reduction of $2,200,000, which means that it wouldn't have to pay interest to borrow that $2,200,000; and that would be a big step forward.

An achievable goal for any company with its management head screwed on straight is a receivables turnover of 8.0, which comes out to be about 45 days' sales in receivables. Of course, if your own receivables turnover is all the way down to 5.0 or 6.0, and if you are charging your customers, say, 2 or 3% a month interest, and if they are paying it, well then that's not a bad deal. On the other hand, if, like Bay, you are paying through the nose for current asset financing, then pick up the phone and ask for the check. And write 500 times: I *will* collect early, I *will* collect early, I *will* . . .

One simple warning about receivables: remember that if your accountant caught your receivables account in an unusual condition when he pulled your statements, then this ratio may be misleading. It's like the old farmer who owed all his money just before the crop came in. A month later, he owed nearly nothing. Watch for distortions like this in any ratio analysis.

If your excess current assets are not in receivables, they will probably be found in inventory somewhere around your company. Your own penchant for "collecting" inventory is measured by ratio 4, inventory turnover, calculated by dividing cost of goods sold by inventory (since

INVENTORY TURNING CAN MAKE LIFE A LOT EASIER...

inventory is shown on the balance sheet at cost, we must compare it with the *cost* of sales; you remember apples to apples). In Bay's case this is $19,100,000 ÷ $7,200,000 = 2.7. OK, how did those other pipemakers do on this one? Wow, we get the booby prize again. No one out there is worse than Bay, Inc., at hoarding inventory. We must be waiting for all that corrugated culvert pipe to turn into valuable antiques. But let's not feel too guilty; let's get to work. After all, someone else out there is doing a fantastic job at turning inventory (15.9 turns a year), equal to about 365 ÷ 15.9 = 23 days' inventory, and I bet they're not geniuses either. But watch it, use common sense. If your accountant showed up to take inventory for this analysis just after you made the largest shipment of your life, then of course he or she is going to find minimum inventory, the level of which *won't* reflect your typical performance.

If Bay, Inc., thought it were tough enough to get its inventory turnover up just to the industry median (6.3), look what would happen. At that point, it would require only $19,100,000 ÷ 6.3 = $3,031,746 in inventory, thereby freeing up $7,200,000 − $3,031,746 = $4,168,254, for which money would no longer have to be borrowed or interest paid.

Bay would love Charlie, a former student of mine. Once in an accounting class the various inventory methods were being discussed; you know, LIFO (last-in, first-out), FIFO (first-in, first-out), and all that good stuff. Charlie volunteered, after looking at the ratios, that it was clear to him that his furniture company had pioneered in the use of a new inventory method: FISH — first-in, still-here.

Using Other Folks' Money
for a Change: Ratio 6

Noninterest-Bearing Current Liabilities to Total Assets: Of course, the way not to borrow any money to run your business (and not to use your own) is to use other people's money — for instance, just like the federal government when it requires you to pay your quarterly income tax declaration or when the government deducts it from a wage earner's weekly paycheck. What a nice way for Uncle Sam to solve *his* financing problems. Well, it's fun to kick the Feds around, but you know and I know they're not alone.

In business, the name of this practice is "leaning on your suppliers," and, yes, there is even a ratio that measures "how well you lean." Look at ratio 6, noninterest-bearing current liabilities divided by total assets. That rather formidable mouthful of words simply gathers together all the current liabilities you owe without paying interest — which is Bay's accounts payable at $4,420,000 — and then divides this figure by total assets — $16,000,000 for Bay. Bay's quotient is $4,420,000 ÷ $16,000,000 = .276, which can be interpreted to mean that Bay, Inc., finances 27.6% of all its assets by using trade credit extended to it by its suppliers. In simple terms, Bay, Inc., "pays late." Remember in computing the "pay late" index, we use only current liabilities on which you are *not* paying interest. When your suppliers start charging you 3% a month to carry you, there is nothing free about that anymore.

Let's look at the "paying late" practices of the corrugated pipe industry. With a median of 13.4%, a top of 29.7% and a low of 2.6% we see quickly that Bay, Inc., is one of the front runners here — not a winner yet, but at least a place or show. (That 2.6% really earns the dunce's award — unless they are getting substantial discounts for paying early.) Of course, you remember the old adage, "Necessity is the mother of invention"; it never applied more than it does to paying late. It's funny how running out of money makes you stretch your payables.

What would Bay, Inc., have to run out of to collect its receivables as well as it stretches its payables? Actually, anything over 20% "free trade credit" is good performance. Most larger suppliers are too well organized and have billing systems that are too effective to permit most people to go much beyond that figure. Bay, Inc., deserves and gets a gold star here for its efforts. Uh, do I hear some polite throat clearing from the back of the room? Well, if you think you deserve a medal, slip in and do a random check of your accounts payable for last week and see if any check went out *before* the due date. Shoot the accountant if it did. Nuff said now — more about this in Chapter 6.

A Ratio That Measures a Whole
Lot of Current Stuff: Ratio 16

Working Capital Turnover: Accountants and financial managers use the term "working capital." It means current assets minus current liabilities and is kind of a float — what you have coming in (short term) minus what you have going out (short term). The nearer your working capital gets to zero, the more trouble is what you've got (coming *and* going). On the other hand, for a while at least, the larger your working capital gets, the easier it is for you to pay your bills. Finally, when you let your working capital become huge (large current assets, few current liabilities), you find yourself with lots of ability to pay whatever few bills do come in, but by the same token you've bought this ability with lots of expensive financing of current assets you really don't need (or if you don't finance, lots of assets earning nothing). A happy medium is just what the doctor ordered. For many well-run manufacturing firms, a happy medium is working capital equal to about one-tenth of annual sales.

People generally talk about working capital by using the working capital turnover ratio, sales divided by working capital, which, if working capital is nothing more than current assets minus current liabilities, can be expressed as:

$$\text{Working capital turnover} = \frac{\text{Net sales}}{\text{Current assets} - \text{current liabilities}}$$

For Bay Area Corrugated, Inc., this is calculated as

$$\frac{\$24,000,000}{\$12,600,000 - \$7,330,000} = 4.6 \text{ turns}$$

Look at the industry ratios. The median is 6.9, the high is 16.1, and the low is 2.3. Ah, slipped by again without winding up on the bottom with our 4.6 turns. Well, no gold stars for us, though. Anything less than 10.0 is not worth crowing about. And, yes, you're very observant; the whole industry here is *not* a sterling performer. I said it, and I'll stand by it: if you can't turn your working capital ten times a year, you just ain't got it.

"So how do you turn it?" Thought you'd never ask! Simple: collect early, pay late, cut inventories, reduce cash — nothing complicated. What it amounts to is a good performance on managing current assets and paying late. "Well, that's hard to do," you say. Well, humbug.

Somebody in the industry got 16.1 working capital turns last year. Probably stayed on the phone collecting, gave good discounts for early payment, used the hell out of free financing (paying late), worked at it like he or she meant it. Sure helps!

Games the Fearless Play: Ratio 7

Long-Term Debt to Equity: The term "leverage" is ubiquitous these days, especially in MBA programs. We love talking about leverage, and we used to say even more about it till interest rates went so high. Unfortunately, the amazing now-you-see-it-now-you-don't arithmetic of leverage pales even with the fastest calculator when interest rates go through the sky. Leverage is using other folks' money to run your business — that is, long-term debt money. (This you pay for.) Leverage refers specifically to the extent to which you substitute long-term debt for your own money (equity). The theory goes something like — all other things being equal — the more of other folks' long-term debt money you use, the less of your own equity you have to use, and therefore the higher the rate of return you earn on your own equity.

That's the theory. In practice it comes out as John's maxim.

John is a wealthy realtor in Chapel Hill who has guided my personal real estate investments for twenty years. For the first ten years, John kept saying to me, "Richard I., if you don't get *some* of your money in that apartment house, the least little wind that comes along will blow your roof off." John wasn't into roof structures; what he meant was that, without some equity money, the payments were so high and the cash flow so low that the apartment couldn't stand anything out of the ordinary (repair expense, for instance) without collapsing financially. I kept assuring John that professors and other cash-poor folks have no choice but to use leverage to the maximum and damn the torpedoes; consequently, I followed the real estate rule for twenty years of buying anything for sale in Chapel Hill that I could buy for nearly nothing down. Of course, John was right, winds did come; but I was right too — so did inflation in property values averaging about 15% a year in investment real estate over twenty years. (And if you only put 10% down, the equity "inflates" at 150% that year).

Bay, Inc., goes in for leverage. Look back at its balance sheet and you'll see that long-term mortgage note payable of $2,800,000; that's all it takes to qualify! The ratio to measure how fearless you are as a user of other folks' long-term money is called the long-term debt-to-equity ratio and is figured

$$\frac{\text{Long-term debt}}{\text{Stockholders' equity}} = \frac{\$2,800,000}{\$5,870,000} = .48$$

which is not too fearless at all. Now a homemade interpretation of .48 is simply that Bay, Inc., uses 48 cents of other people's money in long-term debt for every $1.00 of its own equity money to finance the company. Where does that put Bay in the array of fearless entrepreneurs?

The industry ratio study shows the top long-term debt-to-stockholders' equity ratio of 3.9 (which means that some fearless type uses $3.90 of other folks' long-term money for every $1.00 of his own), a median value of .4, and a bottom of 0 (which implies that there is at least one company with no long-term debt). So Bay, Inc., is about in the middle of the pack.

So What? And Why?

Like everything else there's a good reason to use leverage, that is, raise your own debt-to-equity ratio. That reason is to increase your return on stockholders' equity. Here's how it goes. Suppose you have this little company:

Sales	$1,200,000
Profit before taxes	120,000
Taxes (say, 40%)	48,000
Profit after taxes	72,000
Long-term debt	—
Asset turnover	2.0

127

Assets ($1,200,000/2.0)	600,000
Owners' equity (all assets financed with equity)	600,000

Using these figures, you'd calculate your return on owners' equity (after taxes) as $72,000 ÷ $600,000 = 12%, and your debt-to-equity ratio would be $0 ÷ $600,00 or zero.

Now, 12% after taxes these days isn't the joy it once was, so you get to work and borrow $200,000 (at a 12.5% interest rate) for five years, secured by a note on your plant. Then the picture changes to this:

Sales	$1,200,000
Profits before taxes ($120,000 less interest on note of $25,000)	95,000
Taxes (say, still 40%)	38,000
Profit after taxes	57,000
Long-term debt	200,000
Asset turnover	2.0
Assets ($1,200,000/2.0)	600,000
Owners' equity (since you have put $200,000 debt into the company, you can take out that much equity. . . if you know how to get it out)	400,000

Now, using these new numbers, we calculate your after-tax return on owners' equity to be $57,000 ÷ $400,000 = 14.3%. That's a nice little jump up from the 12% we were making before we introduced leverage, and we've paid for the use of the money too.

More, More!

Now to the greedy part. If a jump from 12% to 14.3% is so good, why not borrow, say, $350,000 more in long-term debt, invest it in the company, drain most of your own equity out of the company, and earn an enormous percentage return on your equity? Answer: it can't be done. The hell it can't! Read the letter on pg. 130 I got a few years ago from a friend of mine in California. With a long-term debt-to-equity ratio of 6.9, that's exactly what he did — took most of his equity out of the company and substituted long-term debt. Is your mouth watering? Would you like to know more?

Well, the rules are simple: (1) you have to find some damn fool who will lend you that much; (2) you have to figure out how to borrow it at an interest rate low enough so that you can afford to pay the interest; and (3) you have to be the type who can sleep nights with this debt-to-equity ratio hanging over your head like the sword of Damocles. That's all! My friend does it well. He's in the oil business, doesn't think too much of the future of the industry — wanted to get most of his money out and found a good deal on rates and terms. He put up the whole company as collateral and systematically drained his equity out (ways to do this without paying it all in taxes coming in Chapter 8). And, not to forget, he earns a nice 109.5% on equity too. Not bad! If you can stand the heat. Unfortunately, the rest of us have to get along with long-term debt-equity ratios a bit lower, but we should at least recognize the potential of well-planned and well-executed leverage plays so we can join the game if one comes along. Remember John's maxim, though: with this leverage, if a little wind comes along it'll blow your roof off! Still want to play the leverage game? More on how in Chapter 6.

Reprise

Running the company well (knowing how to make and sell pipe) brings some pennies down to the bottom line — you know, return on sales and all that good stuff. However, to generate a return on *your money* (the real name of the game unless you were born rich), you have got to run the balance sheet right. And we all know what that means: collect early, pay late, buy less, sell your Transtar, turn your inventory more, and, yes, try a little leverage in your life — you'll love it!

July 24, 1978

Dr. Dick Levin
School of Business Administration
University of North Carolina
Chapel Hill, NC 27514

Dear Dick:

Enjoyed the Seminar you and John put on in San Francisco very much. I thought you might be interested in some of the pertinent Balance Sheet figures and ratios of our business. I should mention that all real estate is outside the corporation.

Annual sales (est.)	$7,300,000
Net profit before taxes (est.)	65,700*
Current assets (June 30, 1978)	721,793
Fixed assets (June 30, 1978)	146,622
Total assets (June 30, 1978)	868,415
Current liabilities (June 30, 1978)	192,453
Accounts payable (June 30, 1978)	643,218
Long-term liabilities (June 30, 1978)	590,600†
Stockholders' equity (Jan. 1, 1978)	60,000
Stockholders' equity (June 30, 1978)	85,362
Net profit before taxes/net sales	0.9 %
Net profit before taxes/net worth	109.5 %
Gross profit/sales (Jan. 1)	7.4 %
Net sales/total assets	$8.41
Net sales/fixed assets	$49.79
Net sales/current assets	$10.22
Collection period	15.8 days
Net sales/inventory	60.8
Long-term debt/net worth	691.9%

*After a nearly unconscionable set of salaries.
†This includes $40,000 serial debentures payable to my father and me in 1985.

SIX

Things Are so Good, They're Awful: How to Keep the Growth Monkey off Your Back

> *The appetite grows by eating.*
>
> *– Rabelais*

DOCTOR, CAN THIS COMPANY
BE SAVED?

I got a phone call a few months back from a gentleman in Georgia who had attended one of my seminars on financial management. "Dick," he said, "I think I have the financial disease you talked about in Philadelphia last month; can you come down here and take a look?" A few weeks after that I took off in N-8213Y from Chapel Hill International Airport (one 3,500-foot runway and two dogs) in a downpour of rain, broke out over the clouds by Sanford, North Carolina, and cruised on down to Georgia under blue skies. When I landed, I found a company that had grown from $4 million in sales to $13 million in just four years and was now in desperate financial straits — read: completely out of money, profits, and bank credit. Things were so good they were awful! Recognizing the symptoms of this disease and treating it effectively are the subject of this chapter.

THE GROWTH MONKEY

Uncle Lou Was Right!

My mother's brother Lou, who owned the Frankfort Unity Grocery Store in Philadelphia, was right. It *does* take money to make money. Uncle Lou knew that way back before cash flow analysis and cash forecasting became popular. If he had just been in the textbook writing business instead of the grocery business, legions of MBA students through the years would have been taught Uncle Lou's law in addition to Gresham's law and Keynes's principles.

Poor Lou. He occupied himself more with slicing bologna than with financial management, so thousands of business owners and managers have had to learn Uncle Lou's law the hard way (which is the way Lou learned it). You know, working so hard, doing so well, selling so many widgets that things are so good they're suddenly bad. Uncle Lou's nephew Dick calls this "getting the growth monkey on your back." The growth monkey digs in hard once he's on there, and he's hell to dislodge. And in case you ever think that bankers help you to tame and feed the growth monkey, forget that nonsense! They only help feed his growing appetite; when he really learns to eat a whole bushel of money a day, bankers often turn the other way, muttering something about "the problems of under-capitalized small business." No, my friend, taming the growth monkey is a hard problem, and mostly you're alone with it.

Uncle Lou's Presidential Address
at Boca

If Uncle Lou were alive today, owner of a 400-store food retailing chain, and giving the Food Retailers Association presidential address at their convention in Boca Raton, he would not stand up and tell them that "it takes money to make money" — that's for ten-year-old nieces and nephews crowding up to the candy counter. No, he would lecture his association on "effective asset management," which is what I'm going to do to you now.

Understanding asset management is a cinch with a couple of diagrams. Think of any business in the whole world — I bet you can't find one that runs without assets. Go ahead, try! "OK," you say, "I know this guy down the street who buys fresh vegetables from the local farmers, moves them in a leased truck to wholesale markets a couple of hundred miles away, sells them for cash, and makes a ton of money. He has no assets at all." Wrong. This guy needs cash to buy veggies, doesn't he? And according to Chapter 2, that's a current asset. And if he reports his financial condition honestly, the lease on his truck should be capitalized on his balance sheet. And sure as hell, if your friend doesn't sell out his entire stock of veggies every night, he has another current asset (inventory this time) carried over for a day. And unless he is really stupid, he probably puts the profits he makes into money market funds (another current asset, see) rather than in his savings account or safe deposit box — and so on. So you see, he has lots of assets after all.

No Exceptions

There just ain't any. All businesses need assets to operate. It's as simple as that, so I'll say it again. You just can't operate a business without assets. Whether you own fifty trucks or not doesn't matter; whether you have a building or not isn't the point; the immutable law of business operation — call it Dick's version of Uncle Lou's law if you like — is that you've got to get your hands on assets to operate a business. If you like diagrams, it goes something like this:

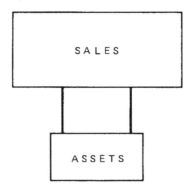

The foundation of any company is its assets, and this foundation will support a given level of sales. When your sales increase, you need a bigger foundation — more trucks, a bigger warehouse, receivables if you trust people to pay later instead of in cash — all the formal trappings of the asset side of the balance sheet from Chapter 2 need to be provided for. So, if your business grows some, then it's sensible to expect your asset foundation to grow some too, looking like this:

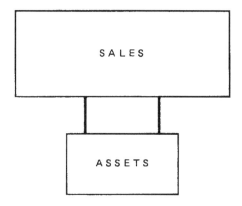

If this relationship weren't true, then, theoretically at least, IBM could have grown to its present size from one office, one truck, one computer, one — well, you know the story. No, Virginia, you simply cannot do it without assets.

Oops, I Think I Got the Rule
Backwards

As long as the assets in your company grow in some rough proportion to the growth in sales of your company, as in the next diagram, you're in fine shape. But heaven help you if this relationship gets out of kilter. If your company looks like this,

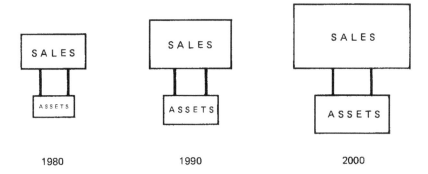

and if the relationship between assets and sales in 1980 was appropriate, you are probably playing the asset management game the right way. But some companies just

135

seem to forget how the relationship should go. If, for instance, your company situation looks more like this,

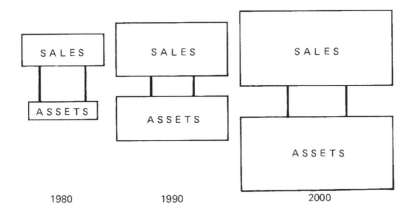

then you just aren't likely to make it till 2000 at all! If this last diagram is you, the growth monkey is really on your back.

Love Your Medium, but What's the Message, Marshall?

The message is that the growth monkey loves to eat, that the food he eats is assets, and that if you don't watch him carefully — read that "exercise the tightest possible financial control over your assets" — he will eat you out of your financial house and home. He will eat you into bankruptcy. "And what does he eat, Coach?" Assets of course! "But what's that to me?" Simple. Assets cost money. And it's either your money (you remember from Chapter 2, "put-in equity" or "left-in equity") or it's other people's money (current and long-term liabilities).

Once More, but Slowly, Please

OK, it takes money to make money. You can't sell from an empty wagon. As your business grows, you need more assets. There are only two ways we know to provide these assets — your money (equity) or other people's money (debt). If the growth monkey is eating you blind and if you keep adding your own money, then pretty soon you will have too much equity in your business and the return you are earning on your equity drops to nothing. If you keep trying to borrow money to pay for the assets the growth monkey eats, pretty soon the interest charges kill you — that is, if your bankers will even lend you enough to feed him in the first place. It's sort of like being allowed to choose between hanging and drowning. You wind up dead either way. "Aren't there any exceptions?" Yes, two. If you are independently rich, then continuing to add excessive amounts of your own money to feed the growth monkey is dumb but possible. Second, if you can find a bank dumb enough to lend you all the money you need to feed the monkey at nearly zero interest rates, you can march on, undaunted.

Some choice, huh? Bankers aren't as smart as folks make them out to be, but they ain't that dumb either! So it really comes down to this: you either control and tame the growth monkey or he kills you. It's you or him. Nothing else works.

THREE DIFFERENT WAYS TO FEED
THE GROWTH MONKEY

Back in Chapter 2, we pointed out that you could provide the assets your company required by using your own money (equity) or by using other folks' money (debt). In actual practice, this issue is a tad more complex than that, so we'll spend a couple of pages here examining in a little more detail ways to feed the growth monkey, both the good ones and the ruinously expensive ones.

More Pictures

What's the best way to provide more assets to a growing business (now that we've agreed you can't do business without them)? Well, consider this diagram:

137

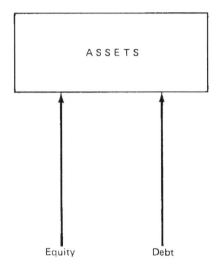

This is the simplest possible way to show how assets are provided. Equity sources represent your money and debt sources represent other folks' money. But, remember, there's debt you pay for and debt you don't — "leaning on your suppliers" we called it in Chapter 5. OK, so we show it this way:

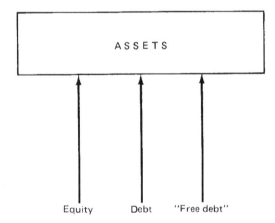

The equity "leg" represents the same source it did in the first diagram; the debt "leg" represents interest-bearing notes, bonds, and so on, the proceeds of which are used to provide assets to the company. The "free-debt" leg is another story — noninterest-bearing trade credit.

Yes, Virginia, There Is
a Free Lunch

Free debt — whatever it is, there ought to be more of it. Sounds wonderful! The proper name for it is non-interest-bearing current liabilities. Free debt is assets provided to your firm on credit but interest free by your suppliers. It is common trade practice to allow customers thirty days to pay their bills; during this thirty-day period, they have the use of inventory (to resell if they can) without paying for it. This is free debt — the use of someone else's capital without paying for it for thirty days.

Look on your own balance sheet in the current liabilities section under the heading "trade accounts payable." That's the money you owe your suppliers, and as long as you *do* pay it during the interest-free period (usually thirty days), you never get charged interest on it; in other words, it's a free loan. And this is no piddling little amount either. It is common to find 25% of a firm's assets financed by free debt. But nothing good lasts long, particularly something as good as free debt. When you fall behind in your payments to the point that your supplier begins to tack on an interest charge to your outstanding balance, it sure ain't free any more. If that interest charge is, say 2% a month, not only is it not free, it's downright expensive debt. Back to Bay. Its balance sheet shows trade accounts payable of $4,420,000. If we assume that these have been kept current (i.e., are not being charged interest), then dividing Bay's trade accounts payable by its total assets gives us something like this:

$$\frac{\$\ 4,420,000}{\$16,000,000} = 27.6\%$$

This means that Bay is providing over a quarter of its assets by the use of free debt — some deal, huh?

Next Picture

Now, if we take the preceding diagram and refine it just a bit, we have the whole picture of where assets come from to feed a growing business:

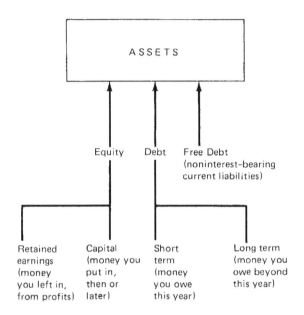

It's still a pretty simple proposition. The three sources of assets are (1) equity, (2) debt, and (3) free debt. Equity is either capital put in before or after you began the business or retained earnings left in after taxes and dividends were paid. Debt is interest-bearing liabilities and is either short term (due within the current fiscal year) or long term (debts payable over a period longer than this fiscal year). Free debt is any noninterest-bearing current liability.

*Diagrams Remind Me of High
School English: Do People Really
Use This Stuff, Coach?*

Last year I ran a financial management seminar at the Hyatt Regency O'Hare in Chicago. In attendance were not only forty manufacturers of a certain product, but six of their major suppliers as well. When we got to the "free-debt" part of the seminar, I decided that a quick and dirty little survey would be useful to make my point. I asked each manufacturer there to calculate his or her own "free-debt ratio" by doing exactly what we just did, this staggering feat of long division:

$$\frac{\text{Noninterest-bearing current liabilities}}{\text{Total assets}}$$

The answers passed up to me ranged from 19.2% all the way up to 38.8%. Someone there was able to finance only slightly more than 19% of assets using free debt, whereas someone else attending financed twice that — almost 40% of assets with free debt. (And I made sure that no one was paying interest on accounts payable to keep this ratio pure.)

This little survey provoked a lively half-hour of discussion on the merits of free debt as a method of financing assets. With both suppliers and purchasers present in the room, we got some interesting slants on financial practices in the industry (in this case, the manufacture of wooden roof trusses). Two of the suppliers volunteered that they each had more than a dozen customers who paid their invoices well *ahead* of time and did so routinely. Now, whether that practice derives from some misguided Victorian model of how to do business or from pure stupidity is not the issue. The issue is that, when used properly, free debt can be a major source of the new assets your business needs to grow — and a *very* inexpensive one, too.

Look at your balance sheet under trade payables; then review your payment practices. If you're not getting the maximum use out of free debt or if you're paying invoices early, call in your accountant and ask him if he knows what free debt is. If you get a stupid look for an answer, I know one way you can reduce your current office expense immediately. Got it?

ASSET MANAGEMENT

Street Talk and Parlor Language

If you haven't guessed by now, most accounting and finance teachers and practitioners too don't go around talking about "free debt," "put-in equity," "left-in equity," and "the growth monkey." This is not considered good form. They use the proper technical terms, which, though precisely defined and consistent, often turn people off from really understanding what good financial management is all about. Let's strike a practical balance and combine some of our home-grown terms with some straight financial balance sheet terminology and address ourselves to asset management — also known as keeping the growth monkey on a diet.

Genesis — Asset Turns

Asset management begins at the beginning—the creation of assets. We already know that you can't sell and grow without assets, so the real problem comes in two parts: (1) where do you get the money to acquire your assets, and (2) how many assets do you *really* need? Chapter 3 suggested where to get the money, so here we go with how many do you need.

The really knowledgeable financial people (not your everyday garden-variety accountants) use the term "asset turns." Of all the financial language of interest to owners and managers of growing businesses, this is the most important, the *sine qua non* (hell, I've got to show off one of the two Latin phrases I know somewhere in this book) of growing successfully, without growing into bankruptcy.

Asset turns are defined as

$$\frac{\text{Sales}}{\text{Total assets}}$$

143

*Bay Area Corrugated Pipe
Revisited — Asset Turns Where
Are You?*

So that we won't dog ear this book by turning back so many times, let's repeat the balance sheet of Bay Area Corrugated Pipe, Inc; we've done this on pages 145–146.

    Using our simple formula, we calculate Bay's asset turns like this:

$$\frac{\text{Sales}}{\text{Total assets}} = \frac{\$24,000,000}{\$16,000,000} = 1.5$$

*Uh, Wonderful,
but Is It Significant?*

Sure. Let's redefine asset turns using one of our home-made definitions (you know, like "put-in," left-in," and "the growth monkey"); then we can show what it means to you and how you can use it.

    The value 1.5 means that Bay Area Corrugated, Inc., gets $1.50 of sales out of every $1.00 of assets it has invested in its company. That is, it has $16,000,000 in assets in the company, and if it has been able to sell $24,000,000 of corrugated pipe in a year on this asset base, then it has been and is able to sell $1.50 of pipe for every $1.00 of assets. This does not mean that Bay can't take another "$1.50 order" for pipe without getting its hands on another "$1.00 of assets." That's silly. It can probably increase its sales a little, say, 5 to 10%, without supplying any more assets. But it cannot grow over time without getting its hands on more assets. Remember, it takes more to make more (Nephew Dick's corollary to Uncle Lou's law).

    If we go back in the financial history of Bay, Inc. — something you can easily do with your own company — and if we find that its assets turns have always averaged pretty near 1.5, then we can say with considerable certainty that over time it needs a dollar of

December 31, 19X2

Assets

Current assets			
Cash	$ 560,000		
Marketable securities	80,000		
Accounts receivable (net)	4,600,000		
Inventory	7,200,000		
Prepaid expenses	160,000		
Total current assets			$12,600,000
Fixed assets			
Land		200,000	
Fabrication shop and office	2,500,000		
Furniture	50,000		
Trucks and machinery	1,700,000		
		4,250,000	
Less: Accumulated depreciation		1,050,000	
Net fixed assets		3,200,000	
Total fixed assets			$ 3,400,000
Total assets			$16,000,000

December 31, 19X2 (Continued)

Liabilities

Current liabilities
Accounts payable	$4,420,000	
Notes payable	1,930,000	
Accrued expenses	280,000	
Long-term note (current portion)	700,000	
Total current liabilities		$7,330,000

Long-term liabilities
Mortgage note payable	2,800,000	
Total liabilities		$10,130,000

Equity

Capital stock		$ 500,000
Retained earnings		5,370,000
Total equity		$ 5,870,000

new assets for each dollar and a half of new sales it's projecting. See, we just turned it around a little, didn't we. Oh sure, Bay can deliver some extra sales with its present truck fleet, and it can probably sell some extra orders out of present inventory, but, again, *over time Bay "chews up" a dollar of assets for each $1.50 of new sales.* If analysis of its past statements indicates 1.5 is the answer, it's as simple as that!

Skin the Cat

Back on the monkey bars, let's climb all the way around in the other direction and look at asset turns again. Our answer — 1.5 — tells us that Bay, Inc., gets $1.50 of sales out of every $1.00 of assets. Suppose now we turn 1.5 upside down — like this:

1.5 upside down $= \dfrac{1}{1.5} =$ .67 (rounded off, of course)

Now what've we got? Well, if 1.5 was previously defined as

$$\frac{\text{Sales}}{\text{Total assets}}$$

then .67 (rounded off) must be

$$\frac{\text{Total assets}}{\text{Sales}}$$

Skeptical? Let's try it:

$$\frac{\text{Total assets}}{\text{Sales}} = \frac{\$16,000,000}{\$24,000,000} = .67$$

Got it?

The .67 means that Bay, Inc., has to get its hands on $.67 of assets for every $1.00 it wants to increase sales. Nothing more complicated than that! OK, we've done it right side up and we've done it upside down — that exhausts the possibilities, there's no other way we can do it!

Love Your Style, but What's
the Application, Coach?

Just watch. Bay, Inc., had sales of $24,000,000 in 19X2; let's let Dame Fortune smile on Southern Florida and predict a 20% increase in Bay's sales for 19X3. The new 19X3 sales level would then be

$$\$24,000,000 \times 120\% = \$28,000,000$$

and using Bay's asset turns of 1.5, we can calculate the level of assets required to support this new sales level as

$$\frac{\$28,000,000}{1.5} = \$19,200,000$$

$$= \text{Total assets required to support 1983 sales}$$

Now, if Bay's assets in 19X2 were $16,000,000, then it would need to come up with $19,200,000 − $16,000,000 = $3,200,000 of new assets for next year. Remember, it could increase sales a little bit without new assets, but nothing like 20%. So if its historic asset turns have been 1.5, then Bay really must find $3,200,000 of new assets next year. Skinning the cat, we could have arrived at the same answer by multiplying .67 times the new sales like this:

New sales = $28,800,000 − $24,000,000 = $4,800,000

New assets required = .67 × $4,800,000 = $3,200,000

So much for the arithmetic; now for the hard part. Our task is to provide those new assets.

Remember, our choices are equity, debt, and free debt. First equity. Bay Area Corrugated earned $420,000 after taxes last year; write that figure down somewhere and keep it for a minute. Now for the free debt. As we showed earlier, Bay, Inc., finances 27.6% of its assets by the use of "free debt" (noninterest-bearing current liabilities); 27.6% of $3,200,000 is $883,200. Write that down too, and we'll add them together:

Last year's profit (after tax)	$ 420,000
Free debt	+883,200
	$1,303,200 (not enough!)

We're short! In fact we are short by

$$\$3,200,000 - \$1,303,200 = \$1,896,800$$

We have used up our equity source (last year's profits after taxes) unless we're willing to buy more stock in our company (i.e., add more put-in equity). We have also used up our free-debt source, which leaves only one other source to make up the $1,896,800. More debt, the kind we pay for.

Suppose that we could find a banker who would lend us $1,896,800. And suppose that the bank would lend it to us on favorable terms (after all, we make a lot of money, says so right on the income statement). Would that solve our asset problem? Read on for the answer.

Falling off the End of the World
with Leverage

Bay's total debt-to-equity ratio (prior to borrowing any more money) can be calculated from its balance sheet like this:

Debt:	
Short term	$ 7,330,000
Long term	+2,800,000
Total	$10,130,000
Equity	5,870,000

$$\frac{\text{Debt}}{\text{Equity}} = \frac{\$10,130,000}{\$5,870,000} = 1.73$$

a fairly hefty debt-to-equity ratio for a company like this. Now suppose that we borrow all the $1,896,800 we need and recompute the debt-to-equity ratio — exactly as a banker would do it *pro forma* before he lent us a nickel:

Debt:	
Existing	$10,130,000
New	+1,896,800
Total	$12,026,800
Equity	5,870,000

$$\frac{\text{Debt}}{\text{Equity}} = \frac{\$12,026,800}{\$5,870,000} = 2.05$$

Hey, now we are *really* in trouble. First, our banker having done this calculation *pro forma* sees a total debt-to-equity ratio of 2.05, far in excess of what our company can safely carry (pay off). Second, he sees the total debt-to-equity ratio *rising* (from 1.73 last year to 2.05 this year). This is a double whammy — two danger signals to a banker. Flags down all over the field. There is not a chance in hell that the bank will come across with the money now. Our financial structure is simply out of control, and we have used up every source of new money except putting more of our own into the business.

Welcome to Exhibit 1, the Achilles heel of smaller businesses, especially of those businesses that haven't mastered asset management. Things are now so *good* — a 20% sales increase forecast for next year — that they're *bad.* We have put in every cent of last year's profits and have borrowed up to the point that banks won't lend us any more money, and we still cannot supply the assets that our growing business needs without increasing the capitalization of the company by putting in more of our own personal/family money. "Well, damn, if we gotta, we gotta — what's wrong with that?" You say, "IBM sells stock, AT&T sells stock, why shouldn't Bay, Inc., sell stock to raise money? What's old Levin raising his blood pressure about?"

*You're from Missouri? So I'll
Show You*

OK, you dig into your personal/family bank account, and you cash in a couple of big CDs, and you take out a mortgage on the building that you and your wife own personally, and you come up with the $1,896,800 you think you'll need next year. All this gets deposited in the company account; in return, you get stock certificates worth $1,896,800. Fair deal? No, it's as lousy a deal as it was in Chapter 4. Let me show you why. Bay, Inc., made a $420,000 profit after taxes on $24,000,000 sales last year or, in percentage terms, 1.75%. Let's assume that you make the same percentage on next year's sales, 1.75%. Then my calculations show you will earn

$$\$28,800,000 \times 1.75\% = \$504,000$$

which is a return after taxes on stockholders' equity of

$$\frac{\$\ \ 504,000}{\$7,766,800} = 6.49\%$$

Remember, you had $5,870,000 in equity, and now you have put in another $1,896,800; total now $7,766,800.

Now why would a person who looks as sane as you take money out of CDs and out of family-controlled (versus corporate-controlled) investments to put in a deal with a rate of return of 6.49%. Dumb? You got it! It's a bad deal financially (6.49% is less than we could get if we went fishing for eels on halves); it's a bad deal in terms of what it does to the family/corporate wealth ratio (remember from Chapter 4 the recommendation to watch this carefully and try to keep it above 50%); and it's a bad deal strategically when you put so much in assets into a single-product business with its financial structure out of control. "But, honey," you say to your spouse, "we have the stock certificates to show for it; it's our money, it's our business, and it's just like putting money in IBM or AT&T." If you believe that, you've finally lost your mind!

OK, OK, OK, Coach, I Just Won't
Sell Any More Pipe Next Year

That's one solution all right, but a damn poor one. There are other ways to skin the cat, several in fact. Before you call in all your sales people and tell them to stop selling, let's do some more simple arithmetic. Suppose you and your spouse decide that you've had enough of this nonsense of putting in the business all you make, all you can borrow, and all you have in personal wealth — feeding the monkey on your back. Suppose you both decide next year you are not going to borrow another cent, will not put into the business another dollar of profits, will not put one more dollar of your personal wealth back into Bay Area, Inc., and are using free debt as much as you can already. What does this mean for asset management?

Biting the Bullet

Try this on. Suppose Bay, Inc., will just have to get along next year on those assets it already has. "Even at the higher level of sales?" you ask. Right, even then! Tightening up the old cinch, that's what you're going to do now, having taken your new financial vows. OK, let's start by figuring out what your asset turns would have to be for you to carry out this New Fiscal Year's resolution. With total assets now of $16,000,000 and total sales forecast next year of $28,800,000, you would need an asset turn of

$$\frac{\$28,800,000}{\$16,000,000} = 1.8$$

to get along on your existing assets. But is that possible? I can't answer that for you because I don't know how good you are at cinch tightening, but I bet you were willing to try when the banker turned you down. What I *can* do is point out what an asset turn of 1.8 involves and let you decide whether you're tough enough to take in the girth a couple of notches.

Hold That Line, Hold That Line

To win, you have to do $28,800,000 sales on the same assets you had this year, $16,000,000. That means that, in the simplest case, every asset account on your balance sheet will have to stay the same next year for you to win. Of course, you could let the levels of the individual asset accounts change as long as the total remained at $16,000,000.

In the next page or so, we will go through the asset accounts one by one, relating them first to a $24,000,000 sales level and then to the higher $28,800,000 sales level, pointing out in each instance the relative difficulty I think a company like Bay would have reaching the goal. As my point of reference, I'll use industry financial ratios just like the ones we got used to in Chapter 5. Let's go through the chart carefully; then you can make up your mind about tightening the cinch. I think you may be surprised.

Will It Hurt Much?

Come on, the comments in the chart (pgs. 154– 155) say that you don't have to be a financial wizard to operate a $28,800,000 corrugated pipe business with $16,000,000 of assets. In fact, it isn't hard at all. What it does take is the proper mindset — read that (1) awareness that the bank is not going to support your monkey's asset appetite any longer, (2) a refusal to put any more of your personal assets in the company, (3) knowledge that increasing your asset turn from 1.5 to 1.8 is rather easy pickin's, an (4) a willingness to watch your cash, collect bills a bit better, sell off some of your inventory, an get into more effective production scheduling in your use of plant and equipment. This calls for concentration, yes, but suffering? Naw!

Asset	Amount	Relative to a $24,000,000 Sales Level	Relative to a $28,800,000 Sales Level
1. Cash	$ 560,000	$\dfrac{\$560,000}{\$24,000,000} = 2.33\%$ A well-run company can get by on 1% of its sales in cash, so Bay's cash account is entirely too high for its $24,000,000 sales level.	$\dfrac{\$560,000}{\$28,800,000} = 1.94\%$ Easy to run with cash equal to this percentage of sales, and
2. Marketable securities	80,000	Unless the return on these is extraordinarily high, or unless we are locked in on a long maturity, or unless they are pledged as security, we should consider them as cash. A surrogate for cash, they are hereby thought of as cash.	if we combine its marketable securities with its cash, we get $\dfrac{\$640,000}{\$28,800,000} = 2.22\%$ which is unacceptably high for Bay.
3. Accounts receivable (net)	4,600,000	This level of receivables is atrociously high and represents $\dfrac{\$4,600,000}{\$24,000,000} \times 365 = 70$ days' sales outstanding. Normal would be something nearer to 50 days' sales outstanding and 50 is not a super performance.	This works out to be $\dfrac{\$4,600,000}{\$28,800,000} \times 365 = 58$ days sales outstanding. It is quite easy to operate with this level of receivables.

4. Inventory	7,200,000	This is also unacceptably high and represents $$\frac{\$7,200,000}{\$19,100,000^*} \times 365 = 138 \text{ days'}$$ sales in inventory (raw materials and finished goods combined). Even in extreme cases, it should be possible to work with a 75-day inventory.	An inventory of $7,200,000 is $$\frac{\$7,200,000}{\$22,924,800\div} \times 365 = 115 \text{ days'}$$ sales in inventory (raw materials and finished goods combined). Getting down to this level should be no problem for Bay, Inc. (if it is into or up to taking in the belt).
5. Prepaid expenses	160,000	This is probably the minimum level of prepaids one would find in a company this size and represents more of an accounting entry than a management decision. If, however, Bay is "paying ahead" for anything other than huge discounts, it is foolish and must stop.	Appropriate.
6. Net fixed assets	3,200,000	According to industry ratios, Bay, Inc., has sufficient plant and equipment, even a little excess, for its current sales level.	Any additions to plant and equipment should be considered through leasing (from family-owned companies) and should only be undertaken after careful study of production-delivery improvement possibilities using current facilities.

*Cost of goods sold for $24,000,000 sales.
÷$28,800,000 × .796 (cost of goods sold).

Time out for a Drink and a Joke

The right mindset is encouraged by law in my state. North Carolina has a law that prohibits the sale of beer on credit. That's right. If you're a beer distributor in my state, you don't have to worry about developing any mindset when it comes to managing your receivables. You collect in cash each time you deliver; the state makes sure that beer credit stays at zero. Now there's something there ought to be a law against!

Play It Again, Sam

Which brings me to one of my favorite inventory anecdotes. The biggest department store in Chapel Hill for years was Sam's. Sam had everything you needed from a pair of spats (nickel, if you remember what they were) to a high silk hat. Merchandise in the aisles, merchandise on the counters, merchandise in the back, merchandise out on the sidewalk, merchandise upstairs, merchandise downstairs — so much merchandise that it was hard to walk. Sam was the butt of half the professors in the business school, in particular one named Clarence, who used Sam's store management methods as the supreme example of how not to practice "modern marketing."

But Sam fooled 'em all, most of all Clarence. Sam borrowed what money he needed at 3%, so financing inventory was no big deal then. Sam also understood taxes and accounting very well, and the relationship between them. His inventory was so huge, so diverse, and so impossible to count that his profits were just about anything he chose to say they were. Sam died a millionaire after a very successful and happy life. Clarence, on the other hand, retired on a professorial stipend, still telling jokes about Sam. Are you laughing, Sam?

Back to Business

"OK," you say, "I follow you on the current assets (cash, receivables, and inventory — I admit I have really been a slob here), but my plant and trucks are another thing. If

156

I'm going to put that much pipe out next year, I desperately need a couple of new trucks next year and a rebuild of my rolling mill, and that's going to add $180,000 to my assets even after the trade-in allowance on the old trucks." OK, big spender, if you need it, you need it, but you can't have it both ways. To keep your total assets at $16,000,000 next year, and still spend $180,000 on new fixed ones, you'll just have to cut your current asset accounts by $180,000. A glance back at the chart shows that shouldn't be difficult at all. All you have to do is cut your receivables from 58 days (nearly two months) down to

$$\frac{\$4,600,000 - \$180,000}{\$28,800,000} \times 365 = 56 \text{ days}$$

Or, if you don't think you can reduce receivables below 58 days (and I don't believe you if you say it can't be done), then you can "operate" on your inventory like this:

$$\frac{\$7,200,000 - \$180,000}{\$22,924,800^*} \times 365 = 112 \text{ days}$$

which is only 3 days less than it would have been. So, you see, spending another $180,000 on fixed assets is no big deal, if you just know (1) that you have to cut somewhere else, (2) where your options lie, and (3) how to do it. And in case you hadn't guessed, the answer to (3) is always "work your tail off."

I'm Still from Missouri — Let's See the Reward

My pleasure. Here we are next year doing 20% more business with a rebuilt mill and two new trucks and still the same $16,000,000 in total assets. What's the big deal? Here's the big deal: (1) you didn't have to put in any more of

---

*$28,800,000 × .796 (cost of goods sold).

your own money, (2) you didn't have to borrow any more from the bank (not that they would have lent it to you in the first place), *and* (3) your after-tax return on stockholders' equity just went up from 6.49% to

$$\frac{\$504,000}{\$5,870,000} = 8.59\%$$

Before you tell me that's still nothing to crow about, let me point out that it's a 32% increase over what you were getting! And now that you know how to do it yourself, there's still plenty of return left to squeeze out that turnip before you have to plant anymore. Hey, this isn't so bad after all!

But When Can I Take Some Out,
Coach?

Got the bug, have you? Just found out how to get the growth monkey off your back, and already you're talking about taking profits out of your pipe plant. OK, follow me. Suppose now that your spouse lays down the law: "Dammit, John, why can't we take last year's profits out of the business and have some fun!" "You mean even after I fix the mill and buy those two new trucks?" "You're darn tootin'!" "Can it be done! Let's see. That means I have to reduce assets below $16,000,000 by the amount of the mill rebuild, the two new trucks, and the profits we're going to take out." That's right — learning fast! Total that all up and you get

$180,000	Mill rebuild and new trucks
+420,000	Last year's profits to be "taken out"
$600,000	Total asset reduction

Now where are we going to cut another asset? By jove, I believe you've got it — current assets? Look at your two biggest ones, receivables and inventory. Just for fun, whack $300,000 off each and see what that leaves.

159

$$\text{Receivables:} \quad \frac{\$4,600,000 - \$300,000}{\$28,800,000} \times 365 = 54 \text{ days}$$

$$\text{Inventory:} \quad \frac{\$7,200,000 - \$300,000}{\$22,924,800} \times 365 = 110 \text{ days}$$

Well, don't ask me "can I do it?" I told you three pages back I couldn't answer that question — I just push the pencil around here. The rest is up to you. Remember, with the proper mindset (and add chutzpah too, will you), 54 days of sales outstanding in receivables and a 110-day inventory is not all that hard. Matter of fact, it won't even get you an award in the pipe industry. Some of those pipemakers operate with 45-day receivables and 55-day inventories. "The hell you say — maybe we can sell a couple of trucks, or stretch out those payables and milk that free debt, or even offer a bigger discount for cash, or pay a few cents more for twice a week delivery of steel." Keep thinking those good thoughts. That's what asset management is all about!

I have a good friend, John, in Raleigh, North Carolina, who is in the gasoline business. John hauls his gasoline from the port of Wilmington, North Carolina, 150 miles away, in a truck so old that people hiss and throw things at it when it passes. Now John spends $300 or $400 a month repairing that old piece of junk, but he won't succumb to what he calls a "Transtar fixation." A Transtar is a super-spiffy truck made by International, all chrome, doodads hanging out everywhere, fancy as hell — and only costs $85,000. But John eschews Transtars, why? "Because," he says, "they impact dysfunctionally on my asset turn goals." (John graduated from Yale University.) In 19X2 John had an asset turn in his company of 8.8. He is heavily leased, gives precious little credit to anyone, hauls gas every day (that is, every day his old truck is running), makes do with nearly no assets, and loves every minute of it. No Transstar fixations for John, no sir-ree.

John does have a condo at Aspen, a 380 SL, and an Aerostar 601-P, which is a beautiful 6 passenger twin pressurized flying machine. "Ah, come on, Levin," you say, "we knew you were pulling our leg with that 8.8 turns figure." Would I do that to you? Nope. It all just depends on where you want your money — in inventory, Transtars, and receivables or in Aspen real estate, 380 SLs, and 601-P Aerostars. (And then there's diddling too!)

SEVEN

If We're Making All This Money, How Come We Never Have Any Cash?

> *I can't help from making money, that is*
> *all.*
>
> *– Helena Rubenstein*

Buy low, sell high — you think that's a miracle of the obvious? Sure it is; everybody from Exxon peddling liquid gold down to the local junior high PTA peddling cookies at a cake sale knows *that*. Collect early, pay late — you would think that's obvious too. But in twenty-five years of teaching and consulting, I've learned that you can *never* say too much about collect early, pay late — it just doesn't come as naturally to most people. So here's more about collect early, pay late, plus Sam's fish cart, and the difference between profit (on paper) and cash (that you clutch in your hot little hand). After Chapter 7, let's hope that collect early, pay late is also miraculously clear and perfectly obvious.

PROFIT VS. CASH FLOW,
FUNDAMENTALS,
AND A FISH STORY

Which Is Which?

If you apply the buy low, sell high maxim successfully, you will eventually report high profits — assuming that you don't let your overhead (and your diddling, too) get out of hand. But reporting high profits has a lot to do with the witchcraft of modern accounting. And sometimes when you're downright brilliant at buying low and selling high, you still run out of cash, which has nothing to do with modern accounting — it just means that there ain't no money in the bank to pay bills. Finding yourself in that embarrassing situation (i.e., telling your creditors your profits are high but you don't have any money to pay them) usually means that you've forgotten to invoke the second part of the maxim (i.e., the collect early, pay late part). Confusing profit with cash flow is easy to do; business

163

people have been doing it for years, always discovering the differences painfully. Clearing up that confusion and giving you some rules to play by is the purpose of this chapter, so here's Rule One: profit is generated by applying the buy low sell high maxim. Cash flow problems are avoided by invoking the collect early pay late part. This advice is so good you ought to do it in cross-stitch and frame it.

Who Started All This Trouble Anyhow?

Way back when life was simple and accounting was counting, there was no real difference between profit and cash flow. Look at this income statement from the year 1911.

Sam's Fish Cart
Took-in, Paid-out
(last year)

Fish sold	$10,000
Less: Fish returned	500
Net fish sold	$ 9,500
Credit given	—
Cash taken in (money put in cigar box)	$9,500
Cost of fish (money taken out of cigar box to pay Ben for fish every morning	6,500
Cost of old newspaper	50
Money taken out of cigar box to pay cop on corner every Friday	100
Bills owed	—
Taxes owed	—
Depreciation claimed	—
Profit from fish business	$ 2,850

Money taken out of cigar box for Sarah (wife) to buy food, clothes, and pay rent ($50/week)	2,600	Reconciliation of business profit, cash flow, cash account with family expenses (mine, not Sam's)
Money left in cigar box	$250	

You see, as long as Sam priced the fish a little higher than he bought them, and as long as he did all his business on a cash basis (even with the cop on Fridays), cash flow was no problem for him. His profit for the year was $2,850, and that was exactly the amount of cash he had accumulated in his cigar box (before he took out the $50 a week his family lived on). Profit was $2,850 and it all wound up as cash in the box. You can't get much simpler than that.

Enter Credit

Sam's business flourished, and by sheer dint of hard work, long hours, and a somewhat inelastic demand for fish that year, he increased his sales to $20,000 a year (and Sarah's household allowance to $75 a week). They moved from the lower East Side up to a nice fourth-floor walkup in the South Bronx. He even bought a new push-cart, with an umbrella yet. And since he knew most of the folks in the neighborhood, he began giving them credit, letting them pay him when they drew their money on Fridays. Most paid on time, a few didn't.

At the end of 1912, Sam got out his stubby pencil and prepared another income statement that looked something like this:

**Sam's Seafood Company
Sales and Expenses
1912**

Fish sold		$20,000
Less: Fish returned		1,000
Net fish sold		$19,000
Credit given	$4,000	
Credit paid	$3,000	

165

Credit owed	1,000
Cash taken in (money put in cigar box)	$18,000
Cost of fish (money taken out of cigar box to pay Ben for fish every morning	13,000
Cost of old newspaper	100
New pushcart (incl. unbrella)	700
Money taken out of cigar box to pay cop on corner every Friday	200
Bills owed	—
Taxes owed	—
Depreciation claimed	
Profit from fish business	$ 4,000
Money taken out of cigar box for Sarah (wife) to buy food, clothes, and pay rent ($75/week)	3,900
Money left in cigar box	$100

} Reconciliation of business profit, cash flow, and cash account with family expenses (mine, not Sam's)

Enter Morris Schwartz,
Accountant

Sam was no financial wizard. He knew a lot about whiting, pike, and flounder but zip about accounting; he puzzled quite a bit over his situation. Business was terrific, so why was there still only $100 in the cigar box at the end of the year? Yes, business was twice as good but Sam was nearly out of money. "Oh," he said one day, "I got it! It's the money those miserable customers owe me for the fish. That's it." Now Sam was smart, and he began to realize he needed a financial consultant to help him keep track of this growingly complex fish business, so he made a mental note to do something about it next year. In the meantime Sam worked longer hours, sold more fish, traded in his old pushcart on a new bicycle-pedaled pushcart for $900 difference (with an umbrella, of course), and gave more folks more credit. Some paid, more didn't. Sam also raised Sarah's household allowance to $90 a week and promised

Sarah that, if things continued as well as they were now, he would take her to Atlantic City for a week in August (a slow month for fish). Sarah was pleased, Sam was pleased, and Sam's credit customers were pleased (he didn't have much time to collect, and besides he trusted people).

The year finally came to an end and Sam was puzzled again. In the last few weeks, there had been two instances when there was not enough money in the cigar box to pay Ben for the fish. Ben had let it go with a wave of the hand but had suggested that Sam get Morris Schwartz, Accountant, to help him "get his affairs straight." Sam was beginning to realize that he needed help, and Ben's suggestion did the trick for him. He called Morris, who came by the cart, asked Sam a lot of questions, took the cigar box and the receipts in it, and told Sam he'd be back in a week. Sam pedaled on that morning, feeling better about the whole thing. True to his word, Morris Schwartz, Accountant, returned in a week and gave Sam (1) a bill for $200 and (2) these two neatly typed statements.

Mr. Samuel Moss, Fish Retailer
Income Statement
Calendar Year 1913

Fish sold		$30,000.00
Less: Fish returned		1,500.00
Net fish sold		$28,500.00
Expenses		
Supplies for resale	$19,500.00	
Wrapping supplies	150.00	
Local protection		
consultant	300.00	
Accounting services	200.00	
Depreciation on fixed		
assets	320.00	
Total expenses		20,470.00
Net profit		$ 8,030.00

Mr. Samuel Moss, Fish Retailer
Balance Sheet
December 31, 1913

Assets		
Current Assets		
Cash	$ 50.00	
Receivables	6,000.00	
Inventory	100.00	
Total current assets		$6,150.00
Fixed assets		
Transportation equipment	1,600.00	
Less: Accumulated		
depreciation	−320.00	
Total fixed assets		$1,280.00
Total Assets		$7,430.00

Liabilities		
Trade account payable	1,000.00	
Federal income taxes due	630.00	
Professional services due	200.00	
Total liabilities		$1,830.00

Owners' Equity		
Capital account		
Contributed capital	100.00	
Retained earnings	5,500.00	
Total owners' equity		$5,600.00

"Sam," said Morris, "you are to be congratulated. You have built a nice fish busine.   you made a hell of a nice profit last year — over $8,000. And your balance sheet is strong — nearly $6,000 of equity. Oh, Sam, as soon as you think of it, let me have the $200 for the accounting work, OK?"

Sam was less sanguine about his financial position. "Morris," he said, "you are an educated man. You know how to cipher numbers real good, and you looked at my cigar box for a whole week. How come if I'm doing so

169

well and made over $8,000 in the fish business. I owe Ben $1,000, I ain't been able to pay Sarah the house money for two weeks, and I now owe you $200 and the United States Government over $600?" Morris thought for a moment carefully. "Sam," he said, "it's complicated but I'll lay it out for you nice and simple:

1. I recognized your income on the accrual basis for last year; all the big companies are doing it now, and it makes for a more descriptive set of books, especially now that you are granting credit to your customers.
2. As your business grows and makes more money you need to make provisions for supplying the additional capital it needs. Sam, you are undercapitalized, that's all there is to it.
3. You had not depreciated your assets like you should, so I set up your transportation equipment on a five-year life using straight-line depreciation, with no salvage value.
4. And, Sam, the U.S. Government has just passed what they call an income tax. That's right — they now take a certain percentage of everything you make. I have shown that as a current liability."

Sam was now deflated. Not to mention depressed. "Morris," he said, "I look to you for help. What do I need to do to stay in the fish business? It's the only thing I know." Morris answered with great deliberation, "I think you need to go down to the bank and borrow some money, Sam."

Sam and Morris, Reprise

Sam didn't take Morris Schwartz's advice. Instead he went to see his friend Tony. "Tony," he said, "I got this problem with folks who don't pay me for the fish, and it's killin' me. I hear that you deal in collections." Tony (who looked something like a Coca-Cola machine with a head on it) said, "Not to worry, Sam old man. You just give me a dime on the dollar of everything I collect, and I'll take care of your problem right away." Sam knew a good deal when he saw one, and in a month Sam had money in the cigar box again, Ben was all paid off, and Sarah was happy now that her allowance was fully paid up and was looking forward to

the Atlantic City trip in August. Sam put Morris's bill for $200 in the cigar box and promptly forgot about it. Morris waited till the end of the year (fiscal year, of course), then wrote it off as uncollectible. After twenty-five years, Sam owned the largest fish store in the Fulton fish market. He sold only for cash. Morris Schwartz worked upstairs in Sam's place as a bookkeeper — grade IV.

Buchwald, My Hero

Thinking about Sam's fish cart reminds me of my favorite Art Buchwald story . . .

Dalinsky's Drug Store in Georgetown decides to merge with Fischetti's Meat Market in Bethesda. Dalinsky and Fischetti can't agree on which name to use, so they call the company The Great American Drug and Meat Company. A stock offering is immediately sold out.

They take over the Aetna Curtain Company, Markay Life Insurance Company, Mary Smith Pie and Bakery Company, Winston Life Preserver Company, Washington Green Sox Baseball Club, the Norfolk (basketball) Warriors, and a bank, another bank, a mutual fund, a fried chicken franchise company, and so forth. In less than three years, their original $55 investment has provided $50 million apiece on paper and control of $3 billion worth of business.

Buchwald concludes, "The only danger is that if either Dalinsky's Drug Store or Fischetti's Meat Market loses the lease on its store, the whole conglomerate pyramid could fall down. When you get right down to it, that's the only part of their business that Dalinsky and Fischetti understand."

DOING IT WITHOUT
THE CIGAR BOX

What Makes It Complicated

To understand in your gut the difference between profit and cash flow, first you've got to understand three things: (1) the accrual method of recognizing income, (2) the effect of collection lags, and (3) the cash flow effect of depreciation expense. Nothing to it once you've got those three. A word about each in turn.

Number One: As Sam found out from Morris, it *has* become the practice to recognize income on the accrual basis, that is, to count as income anything you bill — for income statement purposes at least. Therefore, as soon as you send out an invoice, your accountant generally reflects that as income this month. But since it has not yet been collected, he carries it on the balance sheet as a receivable. Theoretically, it is possible under an accrual system to sell on credit all year, collect nothing, and still show normal profits. In practice, of course, this would be ridiculous, since normal credit terms generate payment within a month. In theory, though, it's possible. For this reason, you must *never* confuse profit with cash. *Profit* is what your accountant ciphers up using rules he has been trained to use in common with everybody else in the accounting industry. *Cash,* on the other hand, is what is left in your cigar box. There's a difference. How big the difference is depends partly on . . .

Number Two: The longer it takes you to collect your bills, the worse your cash situation becomes — and all the merry while you may be making a profit (figured on the accrual basis, of course). If your customers take three months to pay you, then you have a three-month lag between billing and receipt. During this time, of course, your suppliers all want their money, your employees expect to get paid every week, and you need to take something out of the cigar box to live on too. Since you can't pay these folks or yourself with receivables (until they are collected), you experience a cash shortage — the old cash flow problem. The longer you let your customers lag their payments from the time you bill them, the worse your cash flow problem becomes. Unless your balance sheet is unusually healthy, or unless you are unusually rich, you can't play the lagged collections game very long before you're in deep trouble. Banks are not in the business of lending money to folks who never collect their own bills. And, besides, the interest cost would soon eat up your profits, even the paper profits

173

reported on the accrual basis. If you do collect your bills within a reasonable time, however, banks (and other financial institutions) *will* lend you money on your receivables. But even *with* this financing source, excessively long collection lags will eventually bankrupt you.

*How Much Is That Worth
in Dollars?*

Listen, even financial institutions sometimes get collect early, pay late backwards. One such lending institution in my neck of the woods got its liquidities all screwed up and found itself the possessor of a ten-year-old apartment complex with a thirty-year note, which it desperately wanted to get off its books in a hell of a hurry. The lender let it be known in the community that sealed bids would be taken from prospective purchasers; bids should include both price and terms.

A few of us who invest in Chapel Hill real estate figured that the project was worth at least $1,400,000 but decided to play the collect early, pay late game with the savings and loan. We put in a bid for $1,100,000 with the entire note to be paid off within two years. The other bidders (and there were three more) all put in bids near $1,400,000, but with terms ranging from twenty to thirty years. The savings and loan sold us the building. It was simple. They were OK as far as profits were concerned, and since they had foreclosed on the building for a bit more than their mortgage, they didn't stand to lose money. What they did need was *liquidity*. They needed to show that the old mortgage would be wiped clean from the books and fast! We were only too happy to oblige them with our modestly low bid. What happened after the two years? Knew you'd ask that. We converted the building to condos and sold it out for nearly $2,400,000. Had to carry the mortgages ourselves, though.

Number Three: The third element in the cash flow game is depreciation. As we pointed out in earlier chapters, depreciation is a *noncash* expense. That is, you never write a check to anybody for "depreciation." Therefore, when we are thinking about cash flow, we recognize that depreciation expense never "left the company cigar box" as Sam's payments for fish did. For that reason, to find our cash position, we *add depreciation back* to whatever figure our books show as profit. After all, if depreciation expense was deducted to calculate profit and if it was not real money paid to anybody, then in a sense it's still here. OK?

Revealing Numbers

Look at this example involving all three elements, the accrual method of recognizing income, lagged collections, and depreciation:

Sales billed (this month)	$1,000,000
Collections (this month — includes money billed in previous months)	900,000
Expenses (includes $50,000 of depreciation	850,000
Profits this month (before tax) $1,000,000 sales − $850,000 expense =	150,000
$900,000 collected − $800,000 <u>cash</u> payments =	$100,000

OK, that's $150,000 profit on paper and $100,000 in the old cigar box. You seem quite comfortable with that one, so let's complicate it a bit. It's fashionable to refer to "after-tax cash flow" these days. All that means is "what's in the cigar box after you pay Uncle Sam." So here we go with a tax example:

Sales billed (this month)	$1,000,000
Collections (this month — includes money billed in previous months)	900,000
Expenses (includes $50,000 of depreciation	850,000
Profits this month (before tax):	
$1,000,000 sales − $850,000 expense =	150,000
Taxes (our tax rate here is 40%)	60,000

175

After-tax profit:

$150,000 − $60,000   =   90,000

After-tax cash:

$900,000 collected − 800,000 cash
     payments − $60,000 tax paid   =   40,000

Want to check it just to be sure? Easily done with the two-cigar-box method, watch:

In Cigar Box		Out Cigar Box	
Collections	$900,000	Expenses (net of depreciation)	$800,000
		Taxes paid	+60,000
Total in	$900,000	Total out	$860,000

In — Out = $40,000 (see, it *does* match up)

See how easy it really is once you get the whole thing arranged in a simple, orderly format? Sam the fishman would love it!

Speaking of fishmen, the contractor who built my cottage down at the coast is named R.T. R.T. has a five-person carpentry crew consisting of Pap (R.T.'s eighty-year-old father), Otis (R.T.'s brother-in-law), Harry (a preacher from Marshallberg), Benny (R.T.'s son-in-law), and Jimmy Noel (the foreman, who doesn't seem to be related to anyone as far as I know). What does R.T. do? As near as anybody can tell, he signs contracts for the construction work and fishes. You can imagine from that job description that R.T. tends to be somewhat lax in his cash flow practices.

Last summer I asked R.T. if he would build us a half-bath under the house to cut down on the distance from the beach to the john (great when you get to be my age and cuts down on sand in the house too). Well, R.T. sent the "boys" by, and I drew the outline in the sand for them. (They don't build with plans.) A week later the bath was finished. Weeks, then months went by, but no R.T. and no bill. Finally, just last week I got a bill from R.T. for the job, almost a year after he did the work. R.T. is reputed to be Salter Path, North Carolina's most affluent citizen, and you know it's true if he can afford lagging his collections by a year.

If you ask me, I think it has to do with Helen, R.T.'s wife. Helen is into accounting, cash flow, and all those progressive things. She runs a very profitable gift shop in Salter Path — you know, buy very low, sell very high. Helen doesn't give credit to anyone. I think Helen's cash flow supports R.T.'s fishin' and laggin'. The contracting business? Oh, that's a family welfare operation — has nothing to do with business!

Combinations

Profits and cash flow can go in some funny directions, depending on how fast you collect accounts, how much depreciation you take, and how well you control costs in your business. There are four possible combinations of cash flow and profit that we need to look at, situations where

1. There is both profit and cash (hallelujah!).
2. There is profit but no cash (cold comfort).
3. There is cash but no profit (O.K. for a while).
4. There is no profit and no cash (wailing and gnashing of teeth).

The accompanying diagram illustrates each of these situations and has notes on it to help you find your way around.

What was that you said? You like Sam the fishman's cigar-box system better? Can't say I blame you, but these are the four outcomes that *can* happen and you'd best be able to recognize them — before they happen to you, please!

On Paper and in Your Pocket — Four Ways

Profit and Cash

Sales billed this month	$120,000
Collections this month	115,000
Expenses (incl. $10,000 depreciation)	110,000
Profit this month (before taxes)	10,000
Taxes (we are paying 40%)	4,000
After-tax profit:	
$120,000 − $110,000 − $4,000 =	6,000
After-tax cash:	
$115,000 − $100,000 (cash payments) − $4,000 =	11,000

Profit but No Cash

Sales billed this month	$120,000
Collections this month	95,000
Expenses (incl. $15,000 depreciation)	115,000
Profit this month (before taxes)	5,000
Taxes (we are paying 40%)	2,000
After-tax profit:	
$120,000 − $115,000 − $2,000 =	3,000
After-tax cash:	
$95,000 − $100,000 (cash payments) − $2,000 =	−7,000

Cash but No Profit

Sales billed this month	$120,000
Collections this month*	125,000
Expenses (incl. $20,000 depreciation)†	130,000
Profit this month (before taxes)	−10,000
Taxes (we are paying 40%)	0
After-tax profit:	
$120,000 − $130,000 =	−10,000
After-tax cash:	
$125,000 − $110,000 = (cash payments)	15,000

No Profit, No Cash

Sales billed this month	$120,000
Collections this month	90,000
Expenses (incl. $20,000 depreciation)	130,000
Profit this month (before taxes)	−10,000
Taxes (we are paying 40%)	0
After-tax profit:	
$120,000 − $130,000 =	−10,000
After-tax cash:	
$90,000 − $110,000 = (cash payments)	−20,000

*A near miracle, appears about as often as Haley's comet.
†Probably spent all his time collecting instead of watching costs.

WHY WORRY ABOUT CASH

Checklist

Under the no free lunch doctrine, even though it's a lot of work looking after cash flow (for someone, if not for R.T.), paying attention to cash has tremendous benefits for businesses. Here is a quick and dirty list of reasons you should get into the cash forecasting business in *your* company (unless it's a cover-up for a gift shop, that is). Find a couple that suit you and come on in.

1. Knowing what the cash situation is and is likely to be avoids embarrassment — for instance, having to tell those lies like "the check is in the mail." No one, especially bankers, likes it when you run out of money.

2. During hard times, if you know what your cash level is going to be and therefore what your cash needs will be, you can borrow exactly what you need and no more, thereby minimizing interest. With interest rates as high as they have been, minimizing interest should appeal to most folks (not counting R.T.).

3. Walking into the bank with a cash forecast impresses the hell out of bankers. It really does. We teach them all this fancy stuff in MBA programs; then they go out and find hardly anybody who does it the way we taught it. So when you walk in with your cash needs all ciphered up so neat and pretty, they go out of their MBA minds. Listen to this story.

I have this friend, Ritchie, a botany professor, who decided to open a bicycle shop a few years ago. He went down to see Gordon, one of our local bankers, and requested a loan of $75,000. Gordon asked Ritchie for his pro formas (you know, his future income statements, balance sheets, and cash forecasts — all nicely typed columns and rows from here to eternity). "Pro-what?" said Ritchie. "Pro formas," said Gordon, "can't lend you any money without them. Essential for business success, an absolute must." A distraught Ritchie dropped by my office later that day and told his tale. I dragged my PORTACOM computer terminal out from under the desk and dialed up our local time-sharing service on the phone. What do these bikes cost, Ritchie? "About $70." And what will they average at retail? "About $165." And what will you spend a month, and what will be your average collection lag, . . . and so on for a dozen other questions he quickly answered. In five minutes using a PRO FORMA program I had written, I had Ritchie three imposing pages of computer output containing pro forma income statements, balance sheets, and cash budgets by quarter for five years. Full of wild cost and market assumptions to be sure, but neat, precise, and orderly to the letter. Ritchie went back to the bank the next week, and when he showed Gordon the pro formas Gordon nearly died. "Now this is what I call a real business plan!" says Gordon. Horse manure — bad times came on the bicycle business in a year and Ritchie lost his ass. No, sorry, make that half his ass — Gordon paid for the other half.

4. Working up future cash needs avoids surprises. It lets you worry about cash needs at a time when you've got your wits together and not in one hectic horrible moment when somebody tells you that you've just run out. Most of us think better with a little advance notice. Thinking about cash needs is no exception.

5. It is difficult going into the bank just after you've bounced a big one. Your banker doesn't like it at all. It sort of cuts the hell out of your negotiating advantage vis-à-vis amount to be borrowed, interest rate, and repayment schedule. When you show up to cover one, you show up hat in hand and you take whatever terms your banker wants to give you. When you show up two months ahead of time, you can be a real cool dude — turn down the first two offers of terms and still have time to negotiate some more. But never when he knows *why* you're in the bank so early this morning.

PUTTING THE COLLECT EARLY, PAY LATE ROUTINE INTO PRACTICE

More Lists

Collecting early and paying late is a mindset you need to develop. Business schools don't teach it; banks don't teach it; lawyers don't teach it — accountants don't even understand it. Nope, like skiing, like sex, like flying, you have to experience it to get the hang of it, and the more you do it, the easier it is. That's the reward. But the best incentive is pain. Try running out of cash before you run out of your good ideas once or twice — that will make a real believer out of you. OK, so if you've had enough sex, skiing, and flying to develop your mindset, here's another quick and dirty list of ways to implement the collect early, pay late routine.

1. Always pay on time, right on time. Not one damn day early! Mail your bills out so they are postmarked on the last possible day before penalties accrue. Never, never pay early. Once more with feeling: never pay anything early, unless you get one hell of a big discount.

2. Make sure discounts offered to you are worth taking. Cipher up the discount and compare it with the cost of the money you are using to pay it. If it ain't a bargain, make them wait for their money to the very last moment.

3. Don't save up deposits. Make daily deposits to your bank so that the balance is maximized all the time. Dead cash helps no one, least of all you.

4. Consider using a money market arrangement that lets you write large checks on it while it pays you the maximum interest all the while. This is not the same as using some savings account that pays a paltry rate of interest. This is a method for earning money market interest rates on everything. Also, the float is usually longer with these funds. Write all the checks you can here, they take longer to clear.

5. Don't let your banker wrassle you into compensating balances. You know who these balances compensate? The banker, not you. If he lends you money, it's your money, dammit, and yours to use the way you want, too. Compensating balances should have gone out with corsets and stays.

6. Bill customers every day; bill them as soon as you finish up the work. Arrange to bill them when the materials are delivered to the job site before work begins. Never let unbilled work accumulate. Be just like the guy who owns the gas station near the race track in Rock Hill, South Carolina. He sells about 7,500 gallons of gas daily, all for cash, and gets ten days' payment terms from his gasoline supplier. Hell, he is one of the few folks I know who *makes* money off his inventory.

7. Spend a lot of time collecting. It's a simple matter of asking people to pay you the money they owe you. Call folks up and tell them you will be in their area this afternoon and would like to stop by to pick up the check. Rebill ten days after the first bill if you haven't received payment. All the

hundreds of studies that have been done over the last fifty years on collection practices come up with the same finding: the more times you ask for it, the more you get. Ask, ask, and keep asking.

8. Collect by telephone. And don't call without having your spiel all worked out. Be ready to counter any and all possible objections with alternatives of your own. Always pause a few seconds after you have identified yourself; it puts the ball in the customer's court and may provoke an explanation right away. Have counterproposals ready on the tip of your tongue (e.g., "Well, can you let me have a check for half of it if I come by in an hour?"). Concessions like that. Make the customer commit to a repayment plan: if it's not today, then next week, but make him commit. Get to his guilt feelings and let them motivate his commitment to you.

9. Make it profitable for customers to pay you on time or even early. Write it into the contracts you negotiate with them from the very beginning to give it legitimacy. Give discounts for quick payment, and make them attractive. After all, you can add 2 or 3% to the cost of work you do for other folks and they tend not to complain; but when they are chronically late paying you, it puts you out of business.

10. Run a check on checks you write to your ten largest suppliers. Watch for a couple of months to see how long it takes from the time you write the checks until they hit your bank. Develop different check-writing rules for different suppliers; for instance, for the ones that take longer to process checks, mail them theirs later. After all, you can always negotiate an overdraft agreement with your banker on an "as-needed" basis. In the meantime, if your suppliers are obviously inefficient with cash flow, go ahead and capitalize on it.

11. Work up a simple system for estimating cash that will be coming in and cash that will go out in the months ahead; teach someone in your office to use it and demand that they keep it up to date. Rely on it, make your cash judgments based on the information it contains, and think of your cash flow projections as being just as useful as your income statement or balance sheet.

12. Make certain any cash on hand but not needed is invested wisely. If you're not into money market funds with check-writing privileges, then make certain you know the simple definitions and rules of the other short-term investments open to you. In case you don't, here is a short primer on that subject. (Information current as of 1982.)

Investments That Bear Interest

a. Negotiable certificates of deposit are time deposits at a commercial bank; the interest rate for certificates of deposit less than $100,000 is controlled (limited) by the Federal Reserve System, but for any deposit larger than $100,000, the interest rate is negotiable. Maturities range from a month to a year.

b. Commercial paper is short-term promissory notes issued by industrial concerns, finance companies, and the like; examples are Commercial Credit Company and General Motors Acceptance Corporation. Interest rates on commercial paper are higher than rates on U.S. Treasury bills and maturities generally range from a month to nine months. Financial rating organizations like Moody's and Standard & Poor assign safety ratings to most commercial paper.

c. Treasury bills are obligations of the U.S. government and mature in a year or less; generally a new issue of bills is sold each week; these can be purchased through your bank (at issue) or through your broker (at any time); maturities can be from a few days up to a year. Usual minimum amount sold at issue is $10,000.

d. Treasury notes are similar to Treasury bills except that maturities range from two months to seven years.

e. U.S. government agency securities generally offer higher interest rates because some of them carry only the "implicit" guarantee of the government; government agencies that offer these securities include those shown in the accompanying table.

Agency	Maturity	Minimum Denomination	Guaranteed by U.S. Gov't.	State and Local Tax
Banks for Cooperatives	2 wks. to 2½ yrs.	$5,000	No	Exempt
Export-Import Bank	6 mos. to 5 yrs.	$5,000	Yes	Not exempt
Farmers Home Administration	6 mos. to 15 yrs.	$25,000	Yes	Not exempt
Federal Financing Bank	8 mos.	$10,000	Yes	Exempt
Federal Home Loan Bank	1 wk. to 10 yrs.	$10,000	No	Exempt
Federal Intermediate Credit Bank	2 wks. to 3 yrs.	$5,000	No	Exempt
Federal Land Bank	2 mos. to 9 yrs.	$1,000	No	Exempt

183

(Table Continued)

Agency	Maturity	Minimum Denomi- nation	Guaran- teed by U.S. Gov't.	State and Local Tax
Federal National Mortgage Assoc.	3 wks. to 18 yrs.	varies $1,000 to $10,000	No	Not exempt
Gov't. National Mortgage Assoc. (participations)	30 mos. to 14 yrs.	$5,000	Yes	Not exempt
Gov't. National Mortgage Assoc. (pass-throughs)	about 30 yrs.	$25,000	Yes	Not exempt

Which, of course, brings us to the final section of this chapter — how to use a system for estimating cash sources and cash needs in your business.

AN UP-TO-DATE TWO-CIGAR-BOX CASH SYSTEM

They All Give the Same Answer

I care not which cash system you use — which system is the eleventh on a list of three things that you worry about when it comes to cash. The point is only that you pick a system you understand, one that fits the needs of your particular business, one you can teach someone else to use, and one that has a high probability of being kept up. Understandable, appropriate, teachable, useful. Nothing else really counts.

There are at last count more than 611,413 different cash systems to keep track of cash (in and out, you know). I have my favorites, and I'm sure you have yours. The one my friends seem to keep using was designed originally by my friend John of Raleigh, N.C., himself an astute businessman and very successful consultant. John's system has gone through about twelve different versions with eight variations on each (that's more than Paganini ever

dreamed of), and here comes the final version, all gussied up ready for your inspection.

John is John, What Else
Can You Say

Friend John believes in maximum leverage on his balance sheet; therefore, it is consistent that he also believes in and strives to maintain nearly zero cash balances. In point of fact, John likes to end the month with about $2,000 in the bank, which for a $5 million company is not bad at all.

John's Twelve-Month Cash Flow Projection

1. Item	JUN	JUL	AUG	SEPT
2. Beginning cash balance (without borrowing)	40,480	21,334	26,585	11,618
3. Projected profits (before taxes)	3,259	5,959	5,741	7,560
4. Taxes (income)	(9,697)	0	0	(7,478)
5. Depreciation	1,400	1,400	1,400	1,400
6. Capital expenditures	(3,000)	0	0	(6,000)
7. Notes payable	(12,108)	(2,108)	(12,108)	(2,108)
8. Change in accounts receivable	1,000	0	0	(4,000)
9. Change in inventory	0	0	0	0
10. Other	0	0	(10,000)	(10,000)
11. Cash balance in checking account (without borrowing)	21,334	26,585	11,618	(9,008)
12. Balance of any interim loans (total)	0	0	0	11,008
13. Balance on investment	19,334	24,585	9,618	0
14. Final balance in checking account (with borrowing)	2,000	2,000	2,000	2,000

(Are you listening, John?) Perhaps the best way to introduce this system is to show it to you and then review the parts one by one in case these need a bit of clarification or explanation. So here goes.

Legend

Row 2: The beginning cash balance for the month; also, of course, the ending cash balance for the month immediately preceding (unless you robbed a bank between the thirty-first and the first).

Row 3: Projected before-tax profits for the coming twelve months. True, it's only an educated guess, and only last year's financial statements are precise, but as we pointed out in Chapter 2, that precision is often an illusion of certainty too. So do your best and make a pro-

OCT	NOV	DEC	JAN	FEB	MAR	APR	MAY
(9,008)	(6,776)	(3,765)	(28,731)	(25,587)	(17,293)	(518)	12,639
5,940	6,719	11,801	10,852	12,002	8,810	5,865	4,720
0	0	(10,059)	0	0	(17,327)	0	0
1,400	1,400	1,400	1,400	1,400	1,400	1,400	1,400
0	0	0	(3,000)	0	0	0	0
(2,108)	(2,108)	(2,108)	(2,108)	(2,108)	(2,108)	(2,108)	(2,108)
(3,000)	(3,000)	(20,000)	(4,000)	(3,000)	20,000	8,000	8,000
0	0	(6,000)	0	0	6,000	0	0
0	0	0	0	0	0	0	0
(6,776)	(3,765)	(28,731)	(25,587)	(17,293)	(518)	12,639	24,651
				John's maximum loan			
8,776	5,765	(30,731)	27,587	19,293	2,518	0	0
0	0	0	0	0	0	10,639	22,651
2,000	2,000	2,000	2,000	2,000	2,000	2,000	2,000

jection — otherwise go into the ministry; or there is always the government.

Row 4: Quarterly income tax payments that will be due (that is, if your profit guesstimates come out true, too). Since this is a cash outflow, it is shown in parentheses. If a loss is projected and a refund is expected, this is shown on row 4 (without parentheses, silly).

Row 5: Depreciation. As we've said any number of times already, since depreciation is counted as an expense for figuring profits (line 3), but since it isn't actually paid out to anyone, it is a noncash expense and is added back here.

Row 6: Capital expenditures. Thought you'd never ask how you pay for things you buy when you never count depreciation as a cash expense. Well here it is! Whenever you plan to buy a piece of equipment, you indicate so in this row under the appropriate month (in parentheses since this is an outflow). If the $3,000 in this row under June represents only the down payment on the machine, then the other payments would be entered in the appropriate columns later in the year, and the interest would already have been deducted from the profit figure in row 3.

Row 7: Notes payable. Here you enter payments that you are obligated to make on notes owed, both principal *and* interest. After all, cash is cash and that's what the noteholder wants to get paid with. (Interest has already been deducted to figure profits.) Notice again, notes payable is in parentheses — that's the official cash-out notation.

Row 8: Change in accounts receivable. Ah, here's a brand-new wrinkle! Anytime you want to give folks more credit, that takes money — your money — thus it's a use of cash (i.e., you get less). And anytime you *reduce* the amount of your receivables, you generate cash (i.e., you get more). The row 8 entry for June indicates that accounts receivable have been reduced by $1,000 (no parentheses); you got that much from collections. In September, we intend to *increase* accounts receivable by $4,000. Matter of fact, September begins John's busy credit season; he gives more then. Remember to use parentheses in September.

Row 9: Use the same treatment for inventory that you did for accounts receivable. Whenever you intend to increase inventory, show the amount in parentheses, indicating a use of cash. Whenever you intend to bring inventories down, show that in row 9 without parentheses, since it's cash coming in. The zeros in this row all the way across until December show that John's inventory will remain constant until December; at that time he will add to it by $6,000. In parentheses, of course.

Row 10: Other.* This is sort of like a miscellaneous row where you can enter any use of cash you may anticipate or any source of cash you like. The two $10,000

---

*If your accounts payable tend to vary significantly from month to month, then you'd add another row to handle that.

entries in August and September indicate John's plan to take $20,000 out of the business during those two months. (He must be going somewhere — R&R.)

Checking and Savings,
Just Like Down Home

Rows 11 through 14 show John how to keep up with what's in the checking account, what he has to invest, and what he needs to borrow. A few words about each of these rows in turn, then over to you.

Row 11: This is his checking account balance, the cash balance if you please. How did we get it? Simple, we just added up rows 1 through 10 algebraically — you know, letting the pluses and minuses cancel each other. This row is the sum. After all, if you start with your cash balance at the beginning of the month (row 1) and then add and subtract everything you put in and took out, it would be weird if the answer didn't come out to be what you had left at the end of the month, wouldn't it? Cash systems aren't weird, and I wouldn't do that to you.

Row 12: Loans outstanding are shown in row 12. John tells us that he does not anticipate any loans during June, July, and August, but the negative beginning cash balance projected for September 1 of ($9,008) will require a loan of that amount plus $2,000 (if he wants to end the month with a $2,000 positive cash balance). Remember, he's the financial cowboy who does $5 million of business on a $2,000 ending cash balance.

Row 13: Here we keep track of the cash we have invested (not in the bank account). Row 13 always has a positive entry in it whenever the cash balance in the checking account (row 11) is larger than the final target $2,000 balance in the checking account. Putting it another way, when more than $2,000 is in cash forecast, everything over $2,000 is invested for that month. This row shows how much it will be.

Row 14: This is John's target balance in his checking account, always $2,000 as his goal.

189

Finis

OK, there you have it, a simple way to keep up with your cash. One that can be learned quickly, taught easily, used lovingly, and long remembered by all. What did you say — you like the two-cigar-box approach to the collect early, pay late routine? Oh hell, so do I. (Where'd we park the fish cart anyway?)

EIGHT

Now That Your Corporation Made All This Money, How Do You Get It Out and Keep It?

*Even when you make a tax form out on
the level, you don't know when it's
through if you are a crook or a martyr.*

– Will Rogers

A friend, Sammy, lives near me down at the coast. I should point out that, although we both have beach cottages, Sammy's "cottage" cost about half a million dollars and has an elevator. He has more invested in his carport than I do in my whole house. Anyway, like me, Sammy is a man of absolutes; his absolutes change from day to day, but on any given day they're absolute. Maybe it's the *way* he talks, as if he were reading off stone tablets.

The other day walking on the beach he said to me, "Levin, a man is worth about twice what he owes." I told him in that case I was in good shape. A couple of weeks ago he came by where I was fishing and said, "You know, Levin, it is a hell of a lot easier to make money than to keep it." This from a man who waited until he was fifty to go into business for himself and in ten years managed to accumulate a fortune of something near $20 million.

Sammy, I would definitely agree with you. It *is* easier to make it than to keep it, and this chapter is about keeping it. Keeping it from whom? Well, not Aspen condominium brokers, airplane dealers, spouses suing for divorce, bookies, the endowment fund of the local institution of higher learning — the diverse host of folks interested in your bucks whom we might call the private sector. You're on your own with those money grabbers. Here we're talking about the public sector. The IRS.

AN INCOME TAX AVOIDANCE PRIMER*

Try for No Tax at All

Why *not* shoot for the moon first? In fact, it's not a dream but the first cut you always make at tax strategy. A no-

---

*Nothing is as certain as death, taxes, and the U.S. Congress monkeying with the tax laws. Anything you read here was current as of 1982. Beyond that, consult your tax advisor, your astrologer, your kids, or your Congressperson.

tax-at-all situation can be realized, for instance, by refinancing a mortgage on a piece of your business property to generate new cash; since no income is realized, no income tax liability is incurred. Tax-exempt income is another way to achieve zero tax payment. Of course, there is no free lunch here, either, since rates of return on tax-free securities tend to reflect a combination of their tax-free status and the risk-return relationship. But whenever they fit your income needs and tax profile, they make good sense.

Another no-tax-at-all situation occurs when you contribute property to a partnership in exchange for an interest in that partnership. Life insurance proceeds are also free of tax. Actually, the IRS publishes quite a list of items excluded from gross income; here are the sections of the IRS code pertaining to businesses exactly as they appear in the law of the land (as of this writing):

Section 101	Certain death benefits
Section 102	Gifts and inheritances
Section 103	Interest on certain governmental obligations
Section 104	Compensation for injuries and sickness
Section 105	Money received under accident and health plans
Section 106	Contributions by employer to accident and health plans
Section 107	Rental value of parsonages
Section 108	Income from discharge of indebtedness
Section 109	Improvements by lessee on lessor's property
Section 110	Income taxes paid by lessee corporation
Section 111	Recovery of bad debts, prior taxes, and delinquency amount
Section 114	Sports programs conducted for the American National Red Cross
Section 115	Income of states, municipalities, etc.
Section 116	Partial exclusion of dividends received by individuals
Section 118	Contributions to the capital of a corporation
Section 119	Meals and lodging furnished for the convenience of the employer
Section 123	Amounts received under insurance contracts for certain living expenses

193

There it is, IRS fans, their own list of "how to do it to them." Why not spend a few hours, browse through it, find some stuff to irritate your tax professional with.

Putting off Doomsday as Long as You Can

I had a tax advisor named Ike for many years. I didn't make much money, so Ike served more in a "filling out the form" capacity than as a real tax advisor. Whenever we would come to a decision point, Ike was always for paying it now; I on the other hand always preferred the "put off dooms-day as long as you can" strategy. I guess Ike was one of those good guys who never put off till tomorrow what he could do today, but I never saw any virtue, or any real return, in applying that behavior to taxes. When I got out of the 20% bracket I found another tax man, Harold. Harold never pays today what he can pay tomorrow, and *this* kind of legal and financial procrastination is just what the doctor ordered when it comes to tax avoidance.

Deferring taxes — postponing doomsday as I say — lets you have the use of your money up until the point when they "get you." This is no bad deal. One way to defer taxes is to defer income to the future. Deferring income may cause it to be subject to lower tax rates later, some-times due to government policy on reducing taxes and sometimes on your reduced earnings in later years. If, however, you think the government is likely to reverse that policy and if you intend to increase your income up until the day you depart from this world, then remember that there's really no completely free lunch here either.

Death and Taxes

Speaking of the long run reminds me of my mother Minerva Levin's favorite joke about it. Seems a drunk named Sam was sitting in church listening to the preacher prophesy a fiery end to the world in forty thousand years for all who sinned. Sam was a little hard

of hearing and leaned over to his partner and asked, "How many years did he say?" "Forty thousand," was the reply. "Thank God," said Sam, "I thought he said four thousand."

Four, forty, or four hundred years — the tax collectors will get you for some of it in the end. But ain't it fun investing and spending the money and minimizing your liability in the meantime. *General Rule:* Defer whenever you can.

More Deferrals

Gains from what the Feds call *involuntary conversions* — things like claims for theft losses, income received from condemnation proceedings, and the like — can be deferred, rather easily into the next tax year and often far longer into the future. Also, when you exchange property for other property just like it (swaps), under the "like-kind" provisions of the tax law, whatever tax would have been due had you sold the property and not exchanged it is deferred into the future until such time as you actually sell the property. The rule here is swap, don't sell. Keep right on swapping into the sunset — make the Feds wait for those taxes. Hell, maybe they'll have abolished the income tax altogether by the time some of your real estate ever needs to be sold.

The House as Tax Haven

The sale of your residence given your age, tax bracket, and the amount of money you get for it is or can be a major tax act, so watch out for the deferral possibilities here too. They can range from a substantial to a total deferral. Consult your tax professional. Furthermore, sales of most property can be made using the installment method of recognizing income, allowing you to spread out the tax burden way into the future — if you must sell at all, that is.

Divide and Conquer

This maxim is our third strategy for taxpayers too! We will have much more to say about each of these items later on in this chapter. For now, you need to remember just this: there are four legal arrangements that can be excellent money shelters in the tax business if they are understood and used correctly. They are partnerships, trusts, leases (from family-owned leasing companies), and corporations (which are still an excellent way to reduce what you owe the IRS). All four of these arrangements sit on the same strategic tax foundation — that is, if you can divide up a big pile of taxable income into many smaller piles of taxable income, the total tax you pay is generally much less. The cleverer you become in using combinations of these four arrangements, the more you'll save on taxes. (Eat your heart out, IRS.)

Uh Oh, a Cautionary Tale

And speaking of becoming cleverer, let me tell you about my friend Sidney. Sidney was a very successful businessman — income exceeding $200,000 a year — but that apparently wasn't enough for him, so he worked out a deal involving only himself, one of his truck drivers, and a lady who worked in his office. (OK, rule 1 for working out tax diddles like this is work it out by yourself; anyone and everyone else might talk.) The deal involved buying, hauling, and selling certain materials off the company books, and thus off the IRS books too.

To make a long story short, Sidney got in an argument with the truck driver, who talked; the driver's story was later corroborated by the office person, who incidentally kept the books on this clandestine nightmare. Sidney got three things: (1) the best tax attorney in the state, (2) lots of character witnesses, and (3) a year's active duty in some army base in Montgomery, Alabama, for this financial "indiscretion." All was not lost, however. While in prison he took off some weight, improved his tennis game, and worked in the prison library with a lawyer named John who had had something to do with a former president. Rule 2 for staying out of prison: don't be too clever. Illegal diddling is dumb, and prison tennis courts are not kept up as well as you may have heard.

When All Else Fails, Punt

When you've tried tax-free income, deferral, and division of income, and you're plumb out of ideas, then try capital gains. The capital gains tax rules seem deceptively simple — the IRS whacks off a huge portion of what you made as exempt from tax before they sock it to you on the rest. In fact, capital gains law is anything but simple, and the best advice here (as in most tax matters) is to get yourself the best tax advisor money can buy. First class is the only way to travel when you fly the unfriendly skies of the Internal Revenue.

Quick, Coach, More Plays

OK, other things you need to learn in your quickie tax primer include avoiding ordinary income whenever possible. This is the tax killer (i.e., taxed at the maximum rates) and must be avoided like the plague. (Taking a capital gain is one way to avoid ordinary income.) When you do have to take it, try to reduce it.

Recognizing bad debts as fast as possible, even if you have to pay tax later on some you do manage to collect, makes good tax sense. Recognizing losses as soon as you can to get the deduction from taxable income is another must. Depreciation taken on buildings and equipment will help reduce income (but under the 1981 rules, recapture *can* be a deadly trap, so think ahead). And, of course, don't forget leverage. Anytime you can deduct the interest expense *and* use borrowed money to buy yourself a whole lot of depreciation *and* still wind up with a cash flow that doesn't bankrupt you, do it, do it!

Once again, the tax laws are complex, rather like navigating the upper reaches of the Orinoco River. They require a pro. Don't stint on your river guide — there are too many crocodiles out there.

RULES FOR SALARIES, DIVIDENDS, AND BONUSES

The Cardinal Rule

When it comes to compensation paid by your corporation to you, generally most is best. Paying yourself achieves the goal of getting money *out* of the corporation, a quest that all but the most diligent fail at. Remember, what you do not pay out as compensation to yourself (and to those other folks in your family you love and trust) stays in the corporation to come out as dividends. Dividends may be defined as what you pay when you run smack out of every other good idea you ever had. Dividends are paid by the corporation out of *after-tax* income and are not deductible. Dividends are thus taxed twice and therefore are to be avoided. Never pay 'em, ever, no! That is, if you can help it.

Warning: If your goal is not getting money out of the corporation but reducing the tax bite to you *and* the corporation combined, watch out for my rule. (Watch out for any single rule for that matter.) If corporations are taxed at rates less than you are taxed personally, it makes little sense to increase your salary. For example, if your corporation pays taxes only at the 22% rate and if you pay tax at a 50% marginal rate, then why increase your compensation if it would cost you 50% in tax dollars while the corporation pays only 22% in tax dollars? Right — makes no sense. But what if a lot of profits pile up inside the company? If your corporation has an accumulated earnings problem (more on this in a minute, but for now equate it roughly to a bad case of the clap), then it pays you to increase your compensation and get more money out. We'll talk about why shortly.

199

*So What's the Most I Can Pay
Myself, Coach?*

That's the question I get asked more than any other every time I give a seminar on this stuff. The basic rule goes like this: if the compensation taken by you is reasonable, then it is deductible by the corporation; but to the extent that the compensation is held to be unreasonable, it is not deductible and, worse, is taxed to the recipient as a dividend. And dividends equal death by taxes. "Hogwash," you say, "what good is a definition that uses the word reasonable?" Good — you're catching on.

Truth is, there is no formula for determining what is reasonable. But don't panic, there are some good guidelines and a few tricks we can show you.

The IRS looks at "reasonable" as what another person like you would receive for doing about what you do, in another company like yours — same industry, same responsibilities, same work load, similar experience, same-size company. Additionally, the IRS puts the burden of proof on you. Whenever they claim that your compensation is unreasonable, *you* have to prove that it isn't; they do not have to prove it is. Ain't that a beaut! If you like citations and trivia, the landmark case is *Botany Worsted Mills* v. *U.S.* So all they have to say is that you are paying yourself too much. That's it — you then have to prove you aren't; when they say you are, that's accepted as correct, *prima facie*, as upheld by the courts in the *Shield Co., Inc.* case. Comes down to this, friends: if they say your compensation is too high, they are done, and it's your turn at bat.

What's Compensation?

Compensation includes the salary you pay yourself plus bonuses you receive, commissions you earn, and any fringe benefits. Fringe benefits are monies that the company pays into your pension plan and profit-sharing plan as well as your company-paid life insurance, health insurance, and accident insurance. Quite a package when you add it all up. And they do, they do!

*Do I Shoot for the Moon
in Compensation?*

The history of compensation cases brought by the federal government is a curious one. It lacks consistency, and many of the decisions are blatantly contradictory. What you need to do is study these and other cases with your tax professional as a preliminary to planning your own best compensation strategy. If you do that, you will have some guidelines — mind you, *guidelines*, not *the* answer. *The* answer you will have when your case is decided (unless, of course, you decide to appeal).

There are thousands of tax cases on compensation. Here is a list of just a few important ones to (1) give you some idea of what you *can* and *can't* do, (2) demonstrate how complex and inconsistent the whole thing really is, and (3) persuade you that this subject warrants some serious thinking (in advance of a court appearance, please) by you and your tax professional. If your tax professional is not familiar with at least half these cases, first thing you do is fire him! Yep, right now!

Case Reference	What Was Decided
Detroit Vapor Stove Co.	Increasing the volume of business warranted increased compensation.
Danly Machine Specialties, Inc.	Developing a new product warranted increased compensation.
Arthur Lederer Milling Co.	Making up for the loss of an assistant warranted increased compensation.
Bergen Fabrics Corp. (knowledge); *Giles Industries, Inc.* (experience)	Experience, technical skills, and specialized knowledge are significant in determining compensation and are easily proved.
Ox Fibre Brush Co. v. *Lucas*	Low salaries paid when you start up a business can be made up later.
Albert Van Luit Co.	A contingent salary that fluctuated based on a predetermined formula was acceptable (percentage of gross profit or money per unit sold).

(Table Continued)

Case Reference	What Was Decided
Charles Schneider & Co., Inc.	A salary based on a predetermined formula was denied; parties were not dealing at "arms length," were diddling, and the formula when applied took most of the corporate profits.
Pepsi-Cola Bottling Co. of Salina, Inc.	A formula compensation system was held to have become unreasonable over time.
Herbst Dept. Store; Walts, Inc.	An officer's salary that had been increased during the year to absorb profits was disallowed and was recalculated into (1) a reasonable salary and (2) corporate profit.
Superior Wines & Liquors, Inc.	A retroactive salary increase was disallowed when rising profits appeared at the end of the tax year and no dividends were paid.
Philadelphia Knitting Mills, Inc.	Compensation in direct proportion to the officer stockholdings suggests that part of this compensation is for services and part is a distribution of profits in the guise of salary.
Osborne Motors, Inc.	The lack of dividends indicates that part of an otherwise reasonable salary is in fact dividends (the court said this was not true when capital improvements were made throughout the years).
Heyman v. Comm.	The excessive salary of one officer cannot be offset against the compensation of another officer.
Lydia E. Pinkham Medicine Co.	The fact that the total compensation of the group of officers is reasonable is immaterial.

*I Just Don't See How I Can Win,
Coach!*

Maybe so, but it's not time to give up yet. True, the litany of compensation cases suggests inconsistency on the part of the IRS, and true again it's hard to derive rules or policies from the court findings, but coming up is a handy bunch of suggestions that, if followed, put you way ahead of the person who plays the compensation game without a plan. Here they are with a note about each:

1. Always put your salary and bonus plan in the minute books of the corporation; state what your official duties are for which you're being paid. The minute book has stature under the law and can be used effectively in court. Take the time to vote on it, and enter it right then, not two years later in your lawyer's office.

2. Never try to develop a compensation plan based on profits. This is easily overturned as avoidance of dividends. Base it on duties, base it on the accomplishment of defined goals not directly related to profits (i.e., raising sales a certain percentage, developing the new sales force, opening up three more states, building the new plant), but *never, never* base it on profits.

3. When you begin the new business, and there is no money to pay large salaries and bonuses, *that's* the time to set up your compensation plan. Then as your business grows and makes more money, compensation will grow automatically, and you never have to change the system you're using. The Feds are particularly adept at seeing through compensation plans that raise your income in good years and lower it in bad years, so don't try anything as foolish as that — the tax on dividends is painful, very painful.

4. Never take bonuses and salaries in "stockholder ratio," that is, in the same ratio as the corporation stock is owned. That is a blatant attempt to avoid payment of dividends and will cost you money *when* — not if — they find you.

5. Never wipe out all your profits with salaries. That is another blatant attempt to avoid paying dividends and is spotted too easily. If you want to cheat, you can do better than that!!

6. Pay dividends every year. "The hell you say! Levin, you talk out of both sides of your mouth — you've been telling us for ten pages that dividends were dumb." Well they are. I said it and I'll stand by it. But I'm talking "penny dividends" here. Always pay a penny or two or even a nickel a share every year. What the hell, so it costs you a couple thousand bucks worth of dividends. You *do* prove to the IRS that you have an unbroken history of dividends, and this is effective in countering arguments that you are trying to avoid them. Look, if you haven't paid any dividends in ten years and they haul you into court and say exactly that, what have you got for a defense? So, think of it as cheap protection; reach into the company coffers and pay a few cents a share every year and save yourself trouble down the road. If paying tax on dividends twice begins to get you (you know, stomach trouble), think of it as an insurance premium!

203

7. Those annual trade association conventions are terrific for tennis, golf, and deep sea fishing, but they're equally good for doing surveys of who pays what salaries. Often the best way to justify the reasonableness of your compensation package, given your duties, is to show that other folks just like you earn the same thing. Do a survey, take copious notes, make copies, let it be reflected in the corporate minute book, be ready to justify your $150,000 salary as president of the Amalgamated Widget Corporation, which does $250,000 annual volume. Go ahead — if you don't ask, you don't get. But check out what those other widget makers pay themselves and make a case for yours truly.

8. And, finally, if you *are* attacked by the IRS for excessively high compensation and you have been in business for a long time, use the consumer or producer price index to defend yourself. Show how rapidly this index has risen over the years and how your compensation package has not kept pace with it (*if* this is true). After all, any index that has risen from a base of 100 to nearly 300 in fifteen years could provide a damn good defense.

GETTING PROPERTY OUT OF YOUR CORPORATION

Don't Get Excited Yet

This is not a way to get appreciated property out of your corporation tax free. Don't be silly, no one knows how to do that, and, besides, who told you to put it in there in the first place? (If you know the answer to that one, shoot the lawyer!) Nope, I said in Chapter 4 that real estate should never (with three exceptions) be put into a corporation, but if you have some in there, read on, we can't save your whole skin, but we may have an idea or two that will save you a couple of pennies.

Dear Old Dad, the Fish Are Bitin'
in Florida

There must be a zillion or so small corporations today that fit these criteria:

1. Dad started the business with an old pickup truck and $1,000.

2. The business is worth a hell of a lot of money today.

3. A fair part of this worth is in appreciated real estate owned by the business (which of course should not have been in the corporation in the first place). This real estate has a low tax base, and to sell it would result in capital gains tax to the corporation and a second tax on dividends if the proceeds were passed out after the sale.

4. Dad is about ready to retire and wants to get his money out of the corporation — all tax free, of course.

To get specific, say that you have a corporation that owns land and buildings worth $1,000,000 that originally cost $200,000. Your father is sixty-eight years old, ready to move to Florida and fish, and owns 60% of the stock in the corporation. Say that Dad's stock is also worth $1,000,000 and we swap him the building and land for his stock. Since the real estate is also worth $1,000,000, we can swap him even. "Great," you say, "but what about the tax?" OK, the corporation pays no tax because it has swapped real estate worth $1,000,000 for stock also worth $1,000,000. But Dad has some capital gains tax liability. His basis in his stock (purchase cost) is only $1,000 plus the old pickup truck (say the whole shebang was worth $5,000). He gets real estate worth $1,000,000 so he has a capital gain of $995,000, on which he will pay about 20% in tax — not nothing, but surely a hell of a lot less than he would have otherwise. And our take isn't over yet. Dad can go to Florida, rent the building to the corporation, use the depreciation on the building to shelter the rental income, and fish to his heart's content. Those of you left behind freezing your asses in Minneapolis can enjoy the fact that you now own the entire corporation (sans land and building of course) and can spend some time planning not to have the corporation buy any more real estate.

The Weather's Beautiful, Wish You Were Here

A couple of final notes on the "Dear Old Dad Real Estate Deal." Not to worry where Dad gets the money to pay the capital gains tax.

An installment sale can be arranged, in which case the tax bite is modest per year. If not, the building can always be mortgaged to pay the capital gains tax. To work this deal Dad has to own 10% or more of the stock and must have owned it for 12 months prior to the redemption, which he did in this case. If the property is worth *less* than the stock, Dad can pay the difference by giving notes to the corporation which he pays over time out of the rent he receives on his building. If the property is worth *more* than the stock, the corporation can put a mortgage on the property to reduce the net value of the property such that it equals the value of the stock. Did you follow all that?

Two points of caution. (1) Get a qualified appraiser, not Cousin Joey, to set the value of the real estate — costs you a couple of bucks but keeps you and the Feds straight. (2) Don't try diddling with the rent Dad charges the corporation when he's down in Florida. Set the rent at the fair market rent for this type of property. After all, you just screwed Uncle Sam out of everything but some capital gains tax dollars (promptly not more than a fifth of the whole profit Dad made on the deal), even though the corporation made a profit when it paid for Dad's stock with the appreciated property. So why be greedy? Remember my friend doing time in Montgomery. Be smart, be legal; if you can't be smart, be dumb, and don't tell anybody what you're up to.

Don't Stop with Dear Old Dad

There is another (legal) trick with corporation-owned real estate you can often pull if you are careful. Suppose this time that the corporation bought some property years ago that has appreciated to many times its purchase price. The family members want to get their hands on the property; they know the law prevents them from buying it from the company at a "bargain," but that doesn't bother them. They want any further market appreciation of the property to accrue to the *family*, not to the corporation. The family is well aware of the attribution rules in Section 1239 of the code, rules that govern the sale of property between husband and wife, or between an individual and a corporation where the individual owns 80% or more of the value of the corporate stock, or between two or more corporations where 80% or more of the value of the stock of each corporation is owned by the same individual. The attribution rules prevent the selling corporation from treating the sale as a capital gain, and the specter of paying income tax at ordinary rates on the enormous appreciated value of the property has kept the family from selling the property.

What to do? Try selling the property to your kids. If you trust them, this keeps the property "in the family" and accomplishes your goal of capturing all further appreciation for the family. "Hell," you say, "my kids can't raise enough money to go to the movies, how can they buy a million-dollar piece of real estate?" Easy, I say, put a $950,000 mortgage on the land and building and lend them a few bucks yourself for the down payment. Then let them rent the building back to the corporation (at market value rents, you slicker, you) so they can pay the mortgage. The corporation pays capital gains rates on their profit (not too bad when you consider it); the kids pay no tax and get control of future appreciation of the property. All you have to watch for here is that they don't sell it next week, take the money, and charter a 747 for five hundred of their friends to attend a rock concert in Melbourne, Australia. (Oh, what the hell, if you have these kinds of problems — real estate *and* kids — there are always trusts, and lawyers to sort out the trusts. But I know some lawyers I don't trust either.)

The Little Buzzards Can Work Too

And if it comes down to the fact that you don't trust your kids with so much money, hell, don't apologize, at least not to me — they're your kids. Put them all on the company payroll to do odd jobs around the place. As long as they're old enough to get a social security card, employing them in your business won't raise the hackles of the IRS and *will* fulfill a major maxim of tax avoidance: taking off the big pile taxed at your marginal tax rate, which is probably 50%, and putting it on little piles, that is, getting it taxed at *their* marginal tax rate, which is probably around 15%.

And if you still have some money in the corporation you'd like to shelter a bit more, set up some preferred stock. This is the kind that never votes, so your kids can't hassle you when you give them some. Then declare a preferred stock dividend from time to time. Sure, you pay tax on your preferred stock dividends too, but the kids all get theirs out at very low tax rates.

Now if you *really* don't trust your kids, even enough for this preferred stock deal, then you have a problem beyond the scope of this book, but I just happen to know a few good family therapists . . . .

Section 1231

Internal Revenue Code Section 1231 was written for the benefit of taxpayers (that's right, I'm not kidding you). It says that if you sell *Section 1231 assets* you've held longer than a year, and if the gains on the sale exceed the losses, then the gains are taxed as capital gains. On the other hand, if the losses exceed the gains, then the losses are ordinary losses. Good deal for you. Gains receive capital gains treatment (lower taxes), whereas losses receive ordinary loss treatment (fast writeoff). Why, thank you. Here's an example. Suppose you own a piece of land with a building on it, and the two look like this:

	Tax Basis	Current Value	Gain (or Loss) If Sold
Land	$50,000	$120,000	$70,000 gain
Building	90,000	40,000	50,000 loss

If you sell them both together, you realize a $20,000 capital gain. If, instead, you sell the building the first year, you declare a $50,000 loss (which you get to deduct right away); then if you sell the land the next year you report a $70,000 profit as a long-term capital gain. "Whoa," you say, "this is nothing more than trading dollars from one year to the next." Not so! Watch.

Suppose that you are in the 50% tax bracket. Then selling the building the first year at a $50,000 loss generates a $25,000 tax saving; selling the land the next year generates a capital gain of $70,000, which let's say is reduced to $28,000 by the 60% capital gains exclusion, and then taxed at 50%, which comes out to a tax of $14,000.

Now do the arithmetic of the sequential sale. A $25,000 saving the first year minus a $14,000 tax the second nets out to plus $11,000. Had you done the deal as land and building in the same year, your tax would have been about $4,000. But by staggering the sales you got off with a gain of $11,000. Not too shabby!

Options, Options, Who's Got
the Option?

Clever person that you are, you got your hands on an option a few years ago to buy an acre in downtown Dallas. The option is now worth a fortune and you are considering exercising it — buying the land and selling it to a developer. Hold it, pardner. If you exercise the option and sell the land next week, you're in trouble; you'll be liable for ordinary income tax on whatever you make. The reason is that under the law you'll have owned the land for one week, not a few years. Better you should sell the developer the option and make the same profit — only this time your gain is a capital gain, and you get off with just a light touch from the IRS.

If I Can't Get the Money out,
by God, I'll Borrow It out or Steal It!

Good for you, shows a lot of spunk! But thievery isn't called for, at least not yet. We have another play or two that may do as well. Enter the *Dean* case. All loans by corporations to controlling shareholders run the continual risk of being called a dividend by the IRS, which means that they get the hell taxed out of them if the charge sticks. The classic case here is the *Dean* case way back in 1961, in which the taxpayer's personal holding company lent him $2,000,000 at no interest. The tax court said that the profit (interest) from an interest-free loan to a controlling shareholder was nontaxable — he didn't have to pay tax on the interest he earned from investing the loan proceeds (which he got for no interest in the first place). "Fantastic," you say, "exactly what I've been waiting for for twenty years. I lend myself $2,000,000 from my corporation (everything but the petty cash account), invest this in tax-free municipals, and presto, I have gotten a hell of a lot of money out." Whoa! The IRS raised hell with the tax court's favorable decision in the *Dean* case — for years and years in fact.

Finally, in 1980 (*Baker*, 75 TC Bo. 11, 1980), the tax court again declared that an interest-free loan was not taxable, even when, in this famous case, Jack Baker used the interest-free loan from his corporation to purchase tax-exempt securities. The *Baker* decision *may* indicate ("may" is the strongest word you should ever use when referring to tax matters) that the IRS is finally fed up with pursuing the *Dean* matter and will leave us all alone from now on to make ourselves interest-free loans from our corporations. Maybe. Only the oracle knows for sure.

With high interest rates, it pays you to take the spare cash out of your business and invest it, leveraged to the hilt, in high-yielding securities — perhaps even in tax-exempt securities. When you did this pre-*Baker*, you could expect a hell of a court fight with the IRS, but the *Baker* case may indicate they're giving up. But if worse comes to worst and the IRS is successful in future court cases in overturning the *Dean* decision, you can always:

1. Set up the loan from your corporation as a real loan, that is, terms, interest (equal to prime we suggest) with a definite repayment schedule.
2. Give yourself a salary increase or bonus (based on services not profits, of course) with which to repay the loan.
3. Tell the IRS to go stick it.

But, until *Dean* is reversed, if ever, go ahead and take the money out as fast as you can in loans. *Just make sure you pay them back before you die;* otherwise you leave your dearly beloved heirs a very sticky estate problem.

BEATING THE EXCESS RETAINED EARNINGS TAX — CREATIVELY

*Laws Is Laws and This One's
a Bitch!*

According to the government, the best way to distribute what a corporation earns is to pay dividends to the stockholders. According to Levin, this is so much B.S. because dividends are taxed at ordinary income tax rates and are taxed twice. So stockholders who are in high tax brackets attempt to get around this by letting the undistributed earnings accumulate in the corporation, where, as you know from Chapter 2, they find their way into the retained earnings account. Since the government understands exactly what game is being played (they also understand my position on this), it provides in Section 531 of the code for a special tax on corporate earnings that have not been distributed. This law applies to all corporations except those that are tax-exempt, personal holding companies, Subchapter S corporations (where the profits have to be passed out every year), and DISCs (domestic international sales corporations, encouraged by the government to foster trade). And since none of these applies to you, the accumulated earnings tax should get your immediate attention.

How Bad Is It, Coach?

Bad, man, bad! The government wants 27.5% on the first $100,000 of accumulated earnings that are excess to the needs of your corporation and 38.5% on all the rest deemed to be surplus to your corporation's needs. (That's as of this writing.) Fortunately (and that's a rare word when speaking of taxes), this exposure is limited to annual income, regardless of how much excess accumulated earnings you have piled up in prior years. Since the statute of limitations applies here too, you are home free except for the last three years, unless you have been fraudulent, that is, lied about your tax liability, and we know you never do that!

Bay Area Corrugated Pipe
Revisited

"I remember them — low asset turns, not much profit, practically no cash, but wait a minute — didn't they have enormous retained earnings on their balance sheet?" Great memory you have. Enormous is right. Try $5,370,000. "Damn!" Yeah, and to make it worse, Bay, Inc., added $4,000,000 of that in the last three years alone. Now this is the stuff promotions of IRS field audit agents are made of. There you are, twenty-six years old, fresh out of MBA school, working on your first assignment with the IRS, Civil Service Grade GS 11, and looking to make a record for yourself. And here comes good old Bay, Inc., with piles of retained earnings and no plan to use them at all! Fantastic! So the IRS takes Bay, Inc., to court and wins. After all, if Bay has no demonstrated plan to use all these damn retained earnings, then they should have been paid out in dividends long ago. "Wait, wait, please," begs the president of Bay, Inc., "you win, Uncle, stop, please, I'll pay them out now as dividends." "No way," says the IRS, "we knew you'd say that, but it's too late, friend. The law won't let you now. No, friend, the way we got it ciphered, you owe us excess accumulated earnings tax on $3,750,000 (they allow you $250,000 without question), which comes to

27.5% on the first $100,000 = $27,500 (the easy part)

38.5% on the rest (i.e.,   = $1,405,250 (the bitter pill)
    $3,650,000)

213

for a grand total of $1,432,750." "Oh shit," you say — what else can you say when the judge says you owe the government $1,432,750 and you have $560,000 in the bank and $80,000 more in marketable securities? Gotcha!

Good Lord — Is There Any
Preventive for This?

Let's hope so. Section 531 court cases are never fought over accumulating retained earnings. Hell, everybody knows it takes a cushion to operate a business, and retained earnings are exactly that. No, the court battles are always over how much cushion is too much cushion. What proportion of earnings represents a cushion beyond the reasonable needs of the business? The key words here are "reasonable needs." It turns out from the Supreme Court *Donruss Company* decision that you can accumulate retained earnings *forever* as long as you can prove by the *preponderance of the evidence* (key phrase, remember it) that tax avoidance was not one of the purposes for the accumulation. Recall that in cases like this the burden of proof is on the corporation, not the IRS. When the taxpayer has no proof of intended use for the retained earnings, he or she is lost. But when the taxpayer can furnish such proof to the IRS, the burden of proof shifts to the IRS. (If you're curious, see the famous *Ivan Allen* v. *United States* case for some good language on this.)

Proof You Want, Proof You'll Get

What is proof? Listen, proof is anything that someone else will believe. Remember when I told you to pay penny dividends every year (nickel a share if you're a high roller)? Well now the reason becomes clearer. A twenty-year unbroken history of dividends is a good place to begin your "proof" that tax avoidance on dividends was not your game. (Total amount is of only secondary importance here; the major point is that you've paid them forever.) So pay those penny dividends, pay them every year, increase them by another penny or two as the company grows, and even to a nickel, but always pay some dividends.

Ain't the IRS Smarter than That?

Sure they are, and paying penny dividends will not win your case for you, especially if you have $5,370,000 in retained earnings. You have got to do more. You need to make a case, a damn substantial one, that you really need the money now or will need it in the future to conduct your business. Arguments that impress the IRS are these:

1. The needs of the corporation are documented in detail in the corporate minute book. (There it is again; that old corporate minute book has stature, at least in the eyes of the IRS, if not in your opinion or your lawyer's.)
2. The corporation demonstrates a need and a plan to expand physical assets — plant and equipment.
3. The corporation has a history of paying dividends — aha, there it is again!
4. The corporation owes money.
5. The corporation is in an industry subject to high obsolescence — it needs to keep moving.
6. The corporation has one, or only a few, customers, raising the risk factor.
7. The corporation *has* gone into a new business in the past.
8. The corporation has a plan to acquire another business and needs money to do so.
9. The corporation has a pension plan it needs to fund.
10. The corporation needs to set up reserves in case of a strike or in case of the loss of its best customer(s).
11. The corporation is involved in a lawsuit and needs to set aside reserves for possible court awards.
12. The corporation intends to acquire the stock of one of its stockholders and needs to set aside funds with which to do this.
13. The corporation needs money to acquire inventories, to carry accounts receivable, and to provide working capital for all of the other needs of an ongoing business.

*Laundry List, How Do I Get It
to Wash?*

Knowing that the IRS is impressed with the items on your list, what you need to do is document, document, document. Let me say that again. Document the hell out of those needs so that they take on an undisputed legitimacy. And the best way I have ever seen to accomplish this documentation in a small company is to hire an MBA student for the summer and instruct him or her to write you a thirty-seven-page strategic business plan with a ten-page appendix of financials (you know, pro formas, those things you use to borrow money from the bank to get in the bicycle business), incorporating as many items on the list as possible. This project will cost you a couple of thousand bucks, but remember, the burden of proof is on you, not the IRS.

The story goes this way. Frank Jones, the fresh twenty-seven-year-old IRS field auditor (with an MBA) walks in and says to Mr. Bay, Inc., "Sir (the IRS instructs all its field staff to be polite), why do you have all these retained earnings; what could you possibly use them for?" Mr. Bay, Inc., replies, "Sir (it pays to be polite with them too), we have given this continuing thought, and we have spent months in serious contemplation of the uses of those funds, and I direct you to our corporate minute book (for the last ten years) in which you will see a carefully thought-out strategic plan for the use of those funds." Now ain't that just a long shot better than some bright reply like "Who the hell are you, what the hell business is it of yours, and where's your warrant?" Or "I don't know what you're talking about, and I ain't saying nothin' till I speak to my lawyer." Or "Kid, what in hell do you know about money?" No, better get a bright MBA for the summer and show her what you want and be ready for the Feds with the thirty-seven-page plan and the ten pages of financial exhibits. When you hit the field auditor with that right up front, it sure makes him consider whether pursuing a Section 531 attack on you is really worthwhile — especially when there are so many other small corporations with *nothing* in their minute books remotely concerned with what to do with $5,370,000.

One final word of caution. Documentation is great, but sooner or later you've got to show that you actually *did* spend some of the $5,370,000, or they will have your ass anyhow. So implement part of your strategic plan (with the ten pages of financial exhibits) every year — not the whole damn $5,370,000, but enough to show movement along that route. If they sue you for the $1,432,750 tax on excess retained earnings we ciphered up a few pages back and they win, you can always work out an installment payment plan with them. They're rather accommodating in this respect, and their interest rates generally lag money market rates by about four percentage points. (Go ahead, cheapskate, get on the horn and call that MBA now!)

NINE

Getting Along with the Pros: How to Use Them Profitably and Sanely

> *I don't want a lawyer to tell me what I*
> *cannot do; I hire him to tell me how to do*
> *what I want to do.*
>
> *– J. P. Morgan*

McKinsey and Company, the respected international consulting firm, once did a study to find out why some computer systems work well and others are a failure. A lot of money and effort went into the study, and when it was over, the findings were deceptively simple. In all the companies studied that had enjoyed success with their computer systems,

1. Top management was deeply involved with the systems. Management did *not* exhibit a hands-off attitude toward the computer — you know, like saying, "I have this marvelous computer person Paula, and I never go near her or worry about what she is doing."
2. Top management demanded planning for the development of the computer operation. Plans were to parallel the company strategy, and performance controls were established for implementing the plans.
3. Top management insisted that the computer operation be staffed with people who understood the business as well as the computer. Letting computer jocks run the computer turned out to be a bomb.

As I think back for years and years on all the sets of books I have pored over at night, all the bank loan meetings I have attended, all the tax fights I have been in, and all the bankruptcies (and near misses) I have been called into, it seems to me that the advice about computers contained in the McKinsey study applies in spades to the whole business of accounting, finance, and taxes. Only, I would paraphrase it this way. In *all* of the companies I know anything about that enjoy a successful and profitable relationship with their accounting, financial, and tax professionals,

1. Top management is literate in accounting and understands the financial system of the company. Top manage-

     ment is a party to any major financial or tax decision made for the company.

2. Top management insists that plans are made for the financial and tax operations of the company, and it makes sure that financial and tax considerations are considered before any strategic decision is made for the company. There's none of this business of "Well, George, I just bought a lumber mill in Conetoe, North Carolina, and merged it into our mobile home wheel plant in Sanford — why don't you fix up the books."

3. Top management will not retain an accounting, financial, or tax professional either on the payroll or on a fee basis who does not understand what business is all about, understand *our* business, understand who *we* are, and understand what *our* financial goals are.

This short chapter will try to persuade you that these three conditions *do* count, that they are highly desirable, and that, if they do not now exist in your company, you *can* bring them about without changing your personality or your life style.

PERSONALITIES

You and Them

You ride a white horse into the dark forest six or seven days a week in search of risky situations — tactical damsels in distress to save, corporate dragons to slay, financial rivers to cross, and tax mountains to climb. Your chief accountant in the next room on the other hand may be a charter member of the green eyeshade fraternity — he may pay his taxes a month ahead of time, keep all his money in the local savings and loan, and arrive at airports at least an hour and a half ahead of every flight. You're happy with who you are, and he's happy with who he is, but that isn't really the question. It comes down to whether you two make sweet financial music together. If so, what he is and his airport behavior are irrelevant. If not just call him up and fire him; right now!

Jerry and Horseflesh

My friend Jerry is a consultant of note in behavioral matters, and I put fairly high stock in most of his advice. Jerry
says that changing the behavior of adults is nonsense.
Can't really be done. If you get to work and bust your ass,
you can make what he calls "about a 15% deviation." I
accept that; Jerry is smart. So he would counsel you
against trying to make an entrepreneurial race horse out
of a good plow nag. (I can't use the silk purse/sow's ear
here — accountants just don't remind me of sow's ears.)
Jerry would say (and Dick would agree), live with the nag
or fire him.

But He Does All the Work,
Coach — and on Time Too!

How do you really know? What is his knee-jerk reaction
when you buy a new piece of machinery and he has to
choose an economic life for depreciation purposes, and
how does he react to charging off bad debts, and is his
conservative view on inventory and cash levels causing
your asset turns to move downward? It turns out that
there are literally hundreds of decisions that your
financial officer makes, most of which you might consider
so routine as not to warrant his or her checking with you.
The financial cost of excessive conservatism is high, but,
make no mistake, so is the cost of excessive error in the
other direction. No, you shouldn't really be able to tell me
you know whether he dots every *i* and crosses every *t* the
way you want it. If you can, you haven't been spending
your time wisely; you're nit picking, watching the pennies
and letting the dollars slip by. What it comes down to is
this. You are either persuaded that your financial officer
thinks like you (or like you want him to think) or you ain't.
If he thinks right, you don't have to watch him all the time.
If he don't think right, get another one, they don't cost that
much.

Chapter 8

YOU GET WHAT YOU PAY FOR

The Mountain View, Georgia
Model

They've probably got a CPA there. They have one in most places, so why not Mountain View, Georgia. Let's call him Harry. Now Harry is a good soul, has a clean practice, doesn't run around, is discreet regarding your financial matters, and goes to Atlanta every November for the state CPA convention. He even serves on one of the committees. Harry audits the books of everyone who's anyone in Mountain View, all the way from the local barber to you, the major industry in town, Amalgamated Mobile Home Wheels, Inc., now selling $8,000,000 worth of wheels annually. Harry subscribes to the Prentice-Hall tax course and reads the booklets they send whenever time permits. He knows a fair bit about financial accounting, auditing, tax, consolidations, mergers, cost systems, and the whole litany they taught him in college. You are his biggest client and he bills you $70 an hour for the work he does and $40 for his "grunts" who actually do your audit. He did all your work (all that your in-house accountants didn't do) last year, and his total bill was $10,400. He gets along well with you, with your in-house accounting staff, with your wife, with your kids, and, for that matter, with everybody who lives in Mountain View. Harry's audits are nearly always done on time, he is a meticulous checker of accounts payable and receivable, and a damn nice fellow.

Thing is, though, Harry is basically your everyday garden-variety auditor-type CPA. Doesn't mean he is ignorant when it comes to taxes and the heavy stuff like that; just means he has to sandwich that specialized knowledge in between everything else he does, including training the grunts in his office and seeing that they all keep their billable hours up each month. You have been bothered a number of times in the past when Harry ended a telephone conversation with "Well, George, I just haven't run into that before — uh, we'll have to see." You are

222

beginning to wonder if Harry keeps track of all the "we'll have to see's."

Uptown Atlanta, Corner Office
in the Sky, Big Eight Model

On the thirtieth floor of one of the new highrises in Atlanta is the office of the tax partner of one of the biggest of the Big Eight accounting firms, Louis. He pulled down $260,000 last year in compensation and bills his time to clients at $210 an hour. He is a good soul, has a good practice, doesn't run around, is discreet, and goes across town to the CPA convention every November. He chairs the tax committee of the national CPA association. He knows a fair bit about the whole litany of accounting subjects he studied at college, but he knows *everything* about taxes — not because Louis is so damn brilliant — he's smart, OK, but that ain't it. It's because he is supported by the firm's twenty-five tax law researchers in New York City, because he is privy routinely to tax rulings partici-pated in by all 1,340 of the tax experts who work for the firm, because he is backed up by the most extensive tax law library on the East Coast, because he has seven tax managers reporting to him, because each of them has five tax accountants reporting to him or her, because Louis has spent twenty-five years studying tax law, tax cases, tax rulings, tax court judges, tax court appeals, and because he has access to everything about taxes that is known by his entire Big Eight firm.

Midtown Los Angeles,
Industry-Specialized Whiz Model

Irving's office is on the sixth floor of the Metro Building in Los Angeles, not a new building but not too shabby either. Irving is a good soul, has a good practice, doesn't run around, is discreet, and goes to the California CPA con-vention every October. He bills his clients $150 an hour and pulled down $140,000 last year. He chairs the state committee on tax. He knows a fair bit about the whole litany of accounting subjects he studied at college, he doesn't know everything about taxes, but he *does* know everything about taxes in the mobile home wheel industry. Irving is what you call an industry tax specialist. His tax practice is limited to an industry (or perhaps a couple of industries), and he knows *everything* about taxes there is to know in that industry. Irving is not backed up by 1,340 tax experts nationally; rather, he has learned what he knows from specializing (which would make Adam Smith happy, I'm sure). He is the tax advisor for forty-three firms in the mobile home wheel industry, represents them when they have to appear in tax court, writes their leases, sets up their real estate and leasing partnerships, and knows more about tax law as it pertains to the mobile home wheel industry than anyone else on earth.

Hold the Models, Give Us
the Rules

The rules are simple. Use Harry for your audits and for your everyday CPA accounting routines. Call up Louis and arrange to spend half a day with him soon. Bring all your tax papers and partnerships and all that stuff. Use Louis to advise you *what* to do, but don't let him do it, he's too expensive. Get the grand plans out of Louis, the overall long-range family/business tax strategy. Then give them to your own local grunt to implement. Next time you hear that Irving is speaking at the annual convention of the Mobile Home Wheel Manufacturers Association of America, get on your horse and go listen to him. If you like what you hear — read that, if he lays at least two ideas on you that Harry and Louis never thought of — then invite him down to your place for a couple of days. Big deal, it'll cost you a few grand but he's a charming guy. Pump him for tax strategy that is peculiar to the mobile home industry — like rulings that affect the members of that industry or tax shelters that come from the way your industry buys parts, puts homes together, and markets them. Drain him of everything he knows that can save you a dime in those two days. Get up early, work his ass off, and keep him up late at night with specific questions. Send him home worn out but still a friend. Take copious notes for Louis and Harry — neither of them knows a damn thing about the mobile home wheel industry.

Reprise

It's nothing different from what you do in your plant. You drive a car to work every morning. You deliver mobile home wheels in your eighteen-wheel Transtar, and you screw around on your days off in your Learjet. Why try to deliver wheels in your car or screw around in your eighteen-wheeler? Nuff said.

Well, I see that we have omitted tax lawyers as an alternative model despite quoting J. P. Morgan at the outset of this chapter. That's not fair. Lawyers follow the same lines as our three models of accountants. There is your everyday garden-variety lawyer like Harry; there is your national tax lawyer like Louis; and then there is your industry specialist like Irving. There are also hybrids and sports too! Depends on whether you like CPAs or lawyers, Gibsons or martinis. You might like, and use, both. Skol!

THE ORIGINAL PYRAMID GAME

Buy Low, Sell High

An accounting firm, or a legal practice for that matter, is a business first and foremost. It has to sell services, take in money, and pay its bills before it generates any profit for the people who own it. The accounting firms you deal with are no different; to be successful, they have to learn how to play the buy low, sell high game. Only, in their case it's bodies they buy and sell.

Enter Jane College, Grunt

Jane has just graduated from college in accounting. She took and passed with high marks the first four parts of the CPA exam. Now all she has to do is two years of professional servitude (called practice) and she will have her CPA designation. So she goes to work for Smith, Smith, Smith and Jones, CPAs in Houston, for a $24,000 annual salary. She and two or three other new grunts report to a "senior," a person who has been with the firm for a few years and who has probably already gotten his or her certificate. The senior is in charge of the work group that goes out to your firm and does the audit. The senior and three or four other seniors report to a manager who has his or her CPA certificate and has probably worked for the firm for five years or so. The manager is in charge of an account; all the work the accounting firm does for you is managed by the manager. The manager and two or three more managers report to a partner. As you may have guessed by the altitude on this pyramid, a partner makes a lot of money.

Now because she has to travel, spend time in the office, study new techniques, go on vacation, be sick, and so forth, only a portion of Jane's time can actually be billed to clients. Accounting firms try to keep this portion high. Near 80% would be nice, but it tends to be a bit less than that, nearer to 70%. Jane also costs her account firm items like retirement, office space, health insurance, FICA, all the goodies — let's say those amount to 30% of her salary. So if you take $24,000 and add 30% of that to it for fringes, you come up with a grand total of $31,200, which is what it costs the accounting firm to keep Jane working. If there are 2,000 potential billable hours in a year, and if the firm bills out Jane for 70% of these, the net cost of having her at the client's place of business or back at the firm doing work for the client is

$$\frac{\$31,200}{70\% \times 2,000} = \$22.29/\text{hour (accurate to two decimal places)}$$

Now watch. As of the writing of this book, no self-respecting public accounting firm would bill a new staff member for less than $40 an hour, and most would be above that. Buy low, sell high — buy for $22.29 and sell for $40.00. That's a markup on cost of 79.45% — not bad. And, remember, all Jane's fringes and time off have already been calculated in the $22.29 figure. So if she is billed out to clients at $40 for 1,400 hours a year, the firm earns a profit on her of

$$(\$40.00 - 22.29) \times 1,400 \text{ hours} = \$24,794$$

or a little over 100% of what they hired her for in the first place.

Jane's Cool, but What's This Got to Do with Me, Coach?

Partners in public accounting firms get a partner's share of the profits, just like Sam's fish cart. The more Janes and Joes they get working and the more hours they bill for Jane and Joe, the higher go the profits, and the higher their income. Now even if a partner bills personally at $210 per hour, that's not the key to riches in this pyramid game, no sir, not at all! Watch the arithmetic, now. Let's use conservative numbers. If every partner manages four managers and if every manager looks after three seniors and if each senior looks after two grunts, then every partner directly oversees the work of forty persons, namely twenty-four grunts, twelve seniors, and four managers. And these are conservative figures. You can figure out the rest for yourself. It is much more advantageous for a partner to work on getting grunts, seniors, and managers working on your books or taxes than working himself on your books or taxes. *Many, many* times more profitable. Come on now, you mean that, when you moved up from selling mobile home wheels on commission to sales manager (with a 2% override on everything that forty salespersons sold), you didn't play the game of passing your old personal customers on to a grunt salesman so you could spend your time more profitably than in direct selling? Of course you did, and it paid off handsomely too. And so it does in the world of public accounting.

So not to be surprised and not to worry when partner Louis in Atlanta tries to pass you on to one of his "brightest associates and a person who knows as much about taxes as I do." He is playing the pyramid game — just like you used to in selling. If what he says is true about his associate (and it may be so), then you get good advice at a lower cost. If, however, the associate will have to run back to Louis to get answers to every question you ask him or her, then you've been had by the pyramid game. If this is the case, confront Louis head on, get it right out on the table up front. "Louis, dammit, I'm paying you $210 an hour for your knowledge and experience in tax matters, and the young man you sent me last week doesn't know diddly about taxes. Now cut out the pyramid game, or I'm just going to go to one of your competitors." And since there are eight Big Eight public accounting firms, there must be seven left you haven't dealt with in Atlanta. See how it goes? Can't blame Louis for trying to make a living — you probably wouldn't expect anything else. Tryin' is tryin'.

MAKING YOUR ACCOUNTING
AND TAX PROFESSIONALS WORK
FOR YOU

The Dog and the Tail —
an Unpleasant Tale

It's rare at one of my financial management seminars if several folks don't come up to me and say, "Dick, I wish I could have you meet our accountant. I've asked him for years if we can do anything different about our tax situation and he still says no." I always feel sad when I hear something like that. It's usually a clear case of the tail

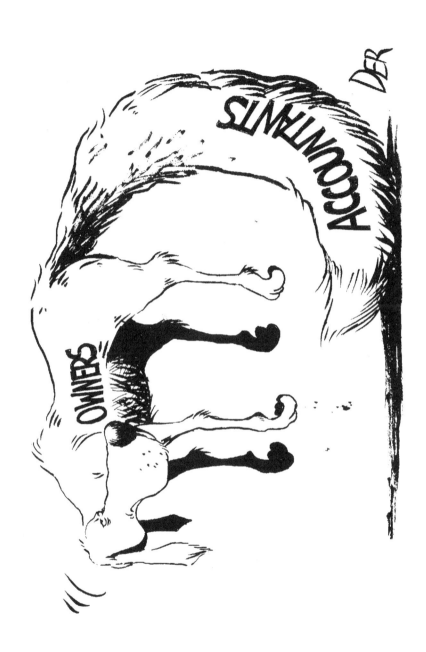

229

wagging the dog. Let's put the same owner who reported that conversation to me into a situation involving one of his plant managers, Charlie. The owner, Sam, comes up to Charlie and asks, "Charlie, why can't we get the welding shop up to standard on mobile home wheel production? I met someone at the convention in New Orleans whose welding shop turns out 25% more than ours." Now, if Charlie replied, "Mr. Sam, we just can't — don't ask me why, and don't ask me to tell you how I know, but we just can't," don't you know that Sam would fire Charlie's ass in five seconds for an answer like that? And yet, don't you also know that Sam sits there and takes the same bullshit from accountants and tax professionals without saying a word? It's downright perverse!

Enter John

I have this friend in Raleigh, John, whom you met in an earlier chapter. John is a good management consultant, was originally and still is a businessman in his own right, running a fair-sized petroleum operation. He deals with Harry, Louis, and Irving, plus tax attorneys of various stripes. John's maxim is never ask an accountant or tax professional "Can we do this?" *Always* ask, "*How* can we do this?" "Do *you* know how we can do this?" "Does anyone else in your firm know how to accomplish this?" "Would someone in another firm know how?" John says those kinds of questions get right to the heart of the matter. John is right, John is also wealthy! See John handle accountants. John is the dog, not the tail.

Never Run a Good Bluff Too Far

You *can* actually ask John's questions even when you don't know a damn thing about accounting or taxation; they will still get interesting reactions. But taking shots in the dark just ain't the uptown way to deal with your in-house and external tax and accounting professionals. No sir, not the right way at all! You shouldn't consider yourself a professional manager unless you know something about accounting and taxes — and I don't mean only what you read in the last eight chapters. This has been a bare beginning, step one. You need to go on. (I wish I could say painlessly, but I can't in good faith.)

So go get yourself enrolled in a good executive course in finance — no silly undergraduate finance or accounting course, but one designed for men and women your age with your responsibilities and with your assets. If you can't find one, get the American Association of Mobile Home Wheel Manufacturers to sponsor one, so all the damn wheel manufacturers can come together, learn something, and at least find out what compensation they pay themselves, so you and they can all diddle the government a bit more. Look at your accounting-finance-tax education as lifelong continuing education, part of your set of executive responsibilities. Right, I know things are always busy and you never have any time, but making money is a damn sight easier than keeping it — on that I think nine out of ten successful business people would agree. And ten out of ten would probably love to do more keeping. Well, you know how to find out how.

A Trash Sweeper Can Only
Do So Much

I know this entrepreneur in South Carlina who runs around buying little businesses. He will land back in his home in Columbia from time to time and alert his accountant to the fact that he has bought another one — all this after the deal is signed, sealed, and delivered. These casual communications of course drive his tax man nearly mad, not because he's afraid of challenges or hard work, no sir, but because doing deals before checking with a tax professional is stupid. It cuts off too many avenues for tax relief that were open at the front end of the deal.

It's said that every good entrepreneur needs a good "trash sweeper" to go around behind him or her and sweep up all the debris, mess, financial havoc, and tax matters that are a part of every deal. It has been my unbroken experience for twenty-five years that bringing your trash sweeper in at the front end of the deal lets him sweep more trash — either out the door or under the carpet — your choice!

Wisdom by Otis

Remember a few chapters back when I told you a little about the crew that built my beach place? Well, this summer Charlotte and I decided to change our unused screened porch into an enclosed sun room. R.T., the contractor, sent Otis and Harry to do the job. Otis is R.T.'s brother-in-law and a fair country philosopher. Otis took me aside one day and said, "Dick, if you'd a thought about this three years ago when we built this house, you'd a saved a right smart bit of money. Dick, when you have ta tear out something and rebuild it, labor is twicest [Down East word for double] what it would a been if you'd a started right." That's as near as Otis has come in three years to criticizing my planning. Inflation has not yet come — as of this writing, thank you Lord — to Salter Path, North Carolina. R.T. charges me just $7.50 an hour for Otis's time, so my planning transgressions come at reduced rates. If, however, you are one of those clowns who has real estate stuck in your corporation, or a million dollars of excess accumulated earnings, or a merged company half of whose carry-back tax loss went unused, listen to Otis and *do it right the first time.* Call in your tax professional, confide in him, trust him, ask his advice, fire him if you like, but don't go rushing off playing entrepreneur without asking him about the tax consequences. It costs too damn much!

Short List to Finish

Winning the finance and tax game is difficult, but the rules are mostly all known. You have to do tax planning — can't run off half cocked and turn a porch into a sun room. You have to know something about accounting and taxes, probably a bit more than you know now, so get to it. You have to find a personality match between you

232

and your accounting and tax professionals. If you don't like them, chances are you can't work with them profitably. You need family/corporate wealth goals — how much, when, and what part inside and what part outside — something for your professionals to work toward. And you need to get used to asking "*how* can we do this," not, meekly, "can we do this?" As Otis always says, "Dick, just tell me what you want it to look like, and I'll build it. You go downstairs and write your books and leave the carpentry to me!" Otis is right. Somebody's got to design the porch so he can build it. That's me and you.

Someday you really ought to meet Otis. He's also very good at gospel music.

Till then . . .

Buy low, sell high, collect early, pay late.

And have fun.

TEN

Ratty Looking Bunch, but They Work Cheap

AUTHOR

Dick Levin is Associate Dean and Professor of Business Administration at the University of North Carolina at Chapel Hill. He's collected several dollars as an engineer, piano player, Air Force officer, teacher, writer, real estate investor, and consultant. And he's paid out a few on planes, boats, apartment houses, and ocean-front real estate. His favorite fixed asset is his Piper Twin Comanche (which *really* moves).

CONTRIBUTING EDITOR

Ginger Travis is a Carolina MBA. This has not stopped her from buying stock options high and selling them low (*very* low). She pays everyone late by instinct, and her lifetime personal best in quick collections is $8.53 taken in a hat while playing as a street musician in Chapel Hill. (It was the most fun, too, until her accountant walked by the hat and made her declare the contents on that year's income tax return.)

CARTOONIST

Lambert Der works as an advertising illustrator in Raleigh, North Carolina. His editorial cartoons appear regularly in *The Raleigh Times* and have surfaced in *The*

Charlotte Observer, The Greensboro Daily News, and *The Chapel Hill Newspaper.* Der refuses comment on his formative experiences with cash flow, but sharp-eyed readers will note the remarkable accuracy of his drawings of U.S. currency and draw their own conclusions.

Interpretation of Statement Studies Figures

RMA recommends that Statement Studies data be regarded only as general guidelines and not as absolute industry norms. There are several reasons why the data may not be fully representative of a given industry:

(1) The financial statements used in the *Statement Studies* are not selected by any random or statistically reliable method. RMA member banks voluntarily submit the raw data they have available each year, with these being the only constraints: (a) The fiscal year-ends of the companies reported may not be from April 1 through June 29, and (b) their total assets must be less than $100 million.

(2) Many companies have varied product lines; however, the *Statement Studies* categorize them by their primary product Standard Industrial Classification (SIC) number only.

(3) Some of our industry samples are rather small in relation to the total number of firms in a given industry. A relatively small sample can increase the chances that some of our composites do not fully represent an industry.

(4) There is the chance that an extreme statement can be present in a sample, causing a disproportionate influence on the industry composite. This is particularly true in a relatively small sample.

(5) Companies within the same industry may differ in their method of operations which in turn can directly influence their financial statements. Since they are included in our sample, too, these statements can significantly affect our composite calculations.

(6) Other considerations that can result in variations among different companies engaged in the same general line of business are different labor markets; geographical location; different accounting methods; quality of products handled; sources and methods of financing; and terms of sales.

For these reasons, RMA does not recommend the Statement Studies *figures be considered as absolute norms for a given industry. Rather the figures should be used only as general guidelines and in addition to the other methods of financial analysis. RMA makes no claim as to the representativeness of the figures printed in this book.* © 1980 by Robert Morris Associates.

Index

CPSIA information can be obtained
at www.ICGtesting.com
Printed in the USA
BVHW031505151021
618877BV00008B/386